Publisher
Safari duha d.o.o.
www.anabucevic.com

Book Design by
Sanja Polovina and Armand Alvarez

Prepress:
Ivan Radić, Mr.Prof.

Copy Editing Consultant by
Vesna Stanković

Armand and Kosta Alvarez Trifunovic
www.weola.one

Cataloguing-in-Publication data available in the Online Catalogue of the National and University Library in Zagreb under CIP record 001156927

ISBN 978-953-49043-2-9

WE ALL ARE ONE: THE ESSENCE OF EVERYTHING THAT EXISTS

A TRANSFORMATIONAL QUESTION-ANSWER DANCE TO EMBODY YOUR FULL POTENTIAL

Armand and Kosta Alvarez Trifunovic

You are about to read an exceptional book.

If it is in your hands, it means you are ready for it. As you will discover by reading it, throughout your life you have asked many questions to which the answers were immediately ready for you. !e only question is whether you were ready for them. Now you are! And you will become aware of it by reading this book. !is book will give you answers to some of the life's biggest questions.

It is a unique experience to read this book at the level of the awareness, on which we have the ability to talk to a universal intelligence available to all of us at all times. !at we can get all the answers when we want. And in this book you will learn how to get them.

I suggest you read it several times. And you will see how with each subsequent reading it will become more and more clear, not only the book, but also how to live this wonderful life, who we really are and how life is really meant to be.

Feel the excitement! You are embarking on a wonderful journey of growth of your soul that will never end....

Ana Bučević
Motivational Speaker, Bestselling Author

TABLE OF CONTENT

From Kosta, with Love 12

From Armand, with Love 18

The First Words 21
The Question-Answer Dance 22
What Is Your Name? 24
We All Are One (WEOLA) 25
Saturday, July 24th, 2021, 11:11 am, Belgrade, Serbia. Weola's Openning 27

CHAPTER ONE | WHO YOU ARE 29

The Perspective of Self 30

- Where are the answers to all the questions being stored?
- Why are some people more balanced than others? What is balance?
- Why do we come to physicality?
- What is the difference between animals and us, nature, and everything else around us?

The Perspective of One 36

- How exactly does the reflection work? Why is there value in it and how can we benefit from it?
- Why is conscious breathing important?
- How does this movement happen? What does movement mean, and what or who moves?

An Integrated One-Self Experience 42

- What is the purpose of the Self and the One?
- What is life?
- What is manifestation?
- What does "the Universe has my back" mean?

CHAPTER TWO | THE BALANCE 49

The Creation Process 50

- What does it mean to observe variety?
- What are thoughts? What is the role of thoughts within the creation process?
- How do I bring the things and experiences I want faster?
- Do I even have to think about what I want?
- How does a question turn into an answer?
- Why do we always want more?
- What does "you are the process" mean?
- Do we observe variety when we sleep, too?

The Question-Answer Dance 62

- What is the question? What is the answer?
- Do we create in both, being in the question and in the answer?
- What are the tipping points?
- Why would I ever want to invite trouble or discomfort?

• How can I be in the question and still feel good?
• What is steadiness?
• What is the role and the difference between motivation and inspiration?
• Does "being" simply mean being present?

The 75-25 Formula 72

• What is reality?
• What is inclusivity? And what are the benefits of it within the experience of life?
• Is the 75/25 formula just for reference?

CHAPTER THREE | THE POWER OF FOCUS 79

The Sense of Survival 80

• Why are we often in survival mode?
• Why are there still people who lack basic resources to cover their survival needs?
• What is fear, and why does fear exist?
• Can the survival mode totally disappear?
• What would you call death and how does it happen?

The Intellect 86

• What is a mirror reflection?
• What is unconditional versus conditional and how does that apply to the creation process?

Living Beyond Emotions 91

• How would you define or describe emotions?
• What is living beyond emotions and how is that process applied to our existence?
• How would you describe Oneness? Do we experience the ultimate satisfaction in that state?

CHAPTER FOUR | YOU INSIDE AND OUT 96

- Do we deliberately choose physical appearance and characteristics like the nose, eyes, etc.?
- How can I affect my genetics?
- What is the Inner Being, and what is its relationship with the body and the mind?
- Where does physical life start?
- Why do explanations coming from different receivers (like Kosta) sound different? Is it the intention of each person receiving?
- Since stretching of the Wider Perspective is limitless, are there infinite angles to flow and share from?
- Can people really lie?
- What is the meaning of ego?
- What is a conscious, and what is a subconscious mind?
- We can access the history. What about predicting the future?

CHAPTER FIVE | YOU AND THE OTHERS 114

- How does the mirror reflection happen?
- When there is someone who is doing something negative, and there is someone that is receiving that negative, how does that work? Are they both a reflection of each other?
- What about the extreme cases? How does that work as a mirror reflection?
- How does mutuality happen? What is mutuality?
- What is the value of different angles?
- What is eternal discovery? Why do we come with different intentions?
- What is the meaning of eternal discovery?
- Does our family choose us, or we choose them, or both?
- How does the choice to be born happen?
- Why specifically do we want to have a life partner?
- What is the essence of the relationship between parents and their children?

CHAPTER SIX | YOU IN THE WORLD **131**

- What is money?
- Do I have to think about the money to have it?
- How do people become multimillionaires or even billionaires?
- How does a person shift their perception from scarcity to experience more abundance?
- What is recognition? Why do we seek it?
- Why do people want to own their own business?
- Why are some steady and some not during a project?
- How does the process between the client and the service work?
- What is the role of expectation within the creation process?

CHAPTER SEVEN | FULL-FLEDGED HUMAN BEING **148**

- Why is the positive state of being more natural to us than the negative?
- Are positive feelings like love, bliss, appreciation, and Divine – static?
- When we want to express ourselves more deliberately, how do we do that?

Weola's Closing **155**
Glossary **156**

FROM KOSTA, WITH LOVE

I have always been extremely curious. Inquisitive really.

Growing up, my parents could never get away with the "do it because I say so" approach to any topic. I was very adamant about wanting to be clear about the "WHY" I was to do whatever I was asked. Talking to my parents as an adult about my childhood, they say there was really no other way but to entertain every single angle I was asking questions from.

I was eight or nine when I had this very memorable moment, which has stayed engraved in my memory. The summer breeze was moving the balcony curtain, as I felt acknowledgment that one day, like everyone else, I will die, too. At first I was upset about it, and fear came over me rather quickly. "How will I not be here forever?" was a question that didn't want to leave my mind. All of this simply didn't make sense.

As I found myself immersed in all the daily activities, this strong feeling softened, and a few days later I had another profound receiving experience. "Everything That Exists is in, and about balance," was the thought that was present and echoing loud and clear. As if treated with a magic eraser, with no contemplation attached, my previously stirred up fear was gone. I felt as though I had broken free to explore the limits of physicality in the only way possible – by questioning everything!

Along the way, my process of wanting to know more would be perceived by others through the lens of confidence, self-love, and often selfishness. Taking care of myself first was a no-brainer growing up as an only child, and quickly became something I was encouraging others to practice without necessarily using words to describe it.

As a consequence, that led to many people confiding in me and often sharing their secrets or struggles. Friends, family members, and rather often – adults! I was equally showered with their stories of their life "wobbles," and with my friends' tales of their adolescent shenanigans. When I think about it from this perspective, it was equally satisfying being around my peers as it was being around mature people full of life experience, who were one or two generations older than me.

I never saw them as any different and wanted everyone to be happy, healthy, successful and as full of love as they could be. It was never satisfying enough to win a competition, or be the best student in class on my own. As I would take care of myself well, I would be able to be there for many of my friends while they were overcoming a tough subject, or for adults, as they were searching for a way to feel better while moving through their tough circumstances.

None of this would have been possible without a foundation we were nurturing at home.

My parents made so many generational context shifts based on their life experiences. They curated an open communication channel I find crucial for being able to allow and receive the wisdom that flows through me, for me and others these days. They have really got it! And because of that, I could soar free even further and broadcast to others the certainty of love coming from that steady, consistent place of our family unit.

So much so that I found myself living in the United States!

First following my dance dream, but more importantly discovering the opportunities for self-growth. Being in New York for many years, a melting pot of cultures, beliefs and opinions – I could not have avoided the stretching of my inclusivity muscle even if I had wanted to. For twelve years, without even noticing, I had been turning within, and step by step, spiritually growing day after day.

Until I met, well, you know who (smiling). Him!!! The world has taken a whole new turn. It has accelerated. The movement towards what we are doing these days got a clear direction when Armand and I met.

Every week I would notice him reading a new self-development book. He loved Oprah Winfrey's *Super Soul Sunday* and would explore everything she was recommending on the show. Armand would share a thing or two here and there, but I was mostly busy dancing and running the dance studio. Since I had never really liked reading anyway, I did not pay much attention to the titles he was bringing home.

Until he recommended, *The Mastery of Love: A Practical Guide to the Art of Relationship: A Toltec Wisdom Book*, by Don Miguel Ruiz. That was the first new age spiritual/self-development material I had laid my eyes on, and it made such an impact that I bought thirty copies and was gifting it to friends, family, and even my bosses! Soon after, my full focus came back to my dancing, and Armand continued to buy book after book.

At one point, I could notice he was becoming overwhelmed, and received the thought it might be from non-stop reading. I told him I was aware he was searching for clarity, but that he might want to give it a rest for some time so he could receive it. He took the advice and stopped buying books for a while.

About a month later, he came home with a seven-hundred-page long, *The Essential Law of Attraction Collection*, Abraham-Hicks edition, three books published as one. All I remember thinking was "This is going to be interesting" (smiling). To my surprise, this was the last book he bought that year! He kept reading it over and over, month after month and occasionally offered me to read it, too.

For six months, it was a "no" from me. Until I was so much under the pressure of not receiving my green card, that I was open to receiving any help to soothe my racing mind. When I opened *The Essential Law of Attraction Collection*, first I skipped through the explanation of the "woo-woo" part about Esther's channeling abilities. I thought that even though it did not make sense, there had to be some great wisdom beyond the weird "spirit interpreting stuff," since Armand stopped searching after finding this book.

As I moved on to read the chapters, one page after another would bring me immense amounts of internal downloads and resonance. It felt as if I was reading and writing this material at the same time. It all made sense.

Evidence from my own life experience was confirming the wisdom written in the book. Halfway through, I had the knowing that all there was for the rest of my life was to become consistent in my deliberate living. One step after another, I "tested out" the intentional living and started seeing small wins along the way. Then I tackled some bothersome old stories (such as the coming out experience) and turned them into fairytale realities.

"Everyone needs to know about this" was the natural next step!

That year, we spent a few thousand dollars on Abraham-Hicks books, gifting them to friends, family, and even random people in the streets of New York. We would share with our inner circle the wisdom we had discovered and were applying, looking for a way to explain the intangible. It took us three years before we discovered a community of like-minded people that traveled while cruising the world together.

Being in an Abraham-Hicks cruise workshop for the first time was an electrifying feeling. Getting familiar with the concept of asking questions in a *hot seat*, in front of more than a thousand people, while receiving the flow beneficial for you and others, was scintillating. And then BEING in the *hot seat* to witness the energy exchange first-hand was an experience like no other.

But only the beginning of a self-discovery journey!

Every further interaction I had with Abraham led me to being closer in understanding and then to the embodiment of what it meant to have an open channel. "What is Esther doing when she is in her: 'quiet mind state' and how does the energy which flows at that moment positively affect everyone who interacts with it? What is in the background of our physical experience and how do all of us have access to the wisdom that seems to be flowing only through a selected few?"

My conversations become more frequent, longer and more profound with each cruise we went on. In March of 2020, the clear message came in one of my *hot seat* interactions with

Abraham: "*We are eager for the hatching of the next stream of questions that will lead to a new stream of answers, whether in a format like this, or directly through your own receiving mechanism.*"

After that exchange, our friends were saying that my eyes had become different. Next day, a huge halo sunbow showed up, a phenomenon I had never witnessed before. I remember being predominantly unfocused for the rest of that trip, basking in this immense energetic upgrade.

FROM ARMAND, WITH LOVE

I guess I have always been a "rebel" in certain ways of thinking, while really loving some traditions that resonate with the way I want to live my life. My curiosity has led me to always wonder if there is something more to me than what I can perceive with my physical senses. Perhaps I have to thank my parents for that, who, although devout Christians, motivated me to question, explore, and discover that my sexuality and physical expression had nothing to do with God loving me or not, but that it was about my own love for myself, beyond what I was perceived to be in the eyes of others.

It seems to me that I have already lived several lives since I was born in Riga, Latvia (then USSR republic), to Latvian-Ukrainian mother and Cuban-Spanish father. We moved to Havana, Cuba when I was four months old, and there I grew up in a bi-lingual environment as I was attending a Russian-speaking school. I remember my childhood in Cuba filled with happy memories, as I was the first child in the family and everyone was happy to be spoiling me. When I turned ten, we moved back to Latvia, which was a cultural shock for me. Later, I could see it was related to a sense of insecurity due to the big shift the whole country was going through after separating from the Soviet Union.

A few years later, embracing my father's Spanish heritage, we moved to Barcelona, where I would live for the next seventeen years. Spain always felt like home and like a culture easy to integrate. I enjoyed living there until I was thirty. The desire to experience a new country and continue learning brought me the opportunity to live in the United States.

Along the way, I switched a ballroom dance studio ownership for an opportunity to study interior architecture in Barcelona, and then work in a New York City based architectural bureau as an interior designer.

The variety of cultures I have been exposed to has naturally made me realize the different perspectives from which I can experience life. I feel I am a CITIZEN OF THE WORLD in its fullest sense. And I embody the feeling of being not only Latvian, Ukrainian, Cuban, Spanish, and as of recently – American, but being it all.

My conscious spiritual journey started when I moved to New York. Through a friend who was an inspirational speaker, I was introduced to self-development literature and Oprah Winfrey's *Super Soul Sunday* show, which instantly became my favorite.

At some point, I was buying and reading every single book by the authors Oprah was interviewing on the show. Soon after, it became an overwhelming feeling to indulge in so many different angles I was exploring through these books at once. At that time, Kosta and I were already living together, and I can still hear his voice telling me, "take a break from reading so much."

And I did. But not for too long. About a month later I was inspired to check out some books at one of my favorite bookstores, Barnes and Noble on the Upper East Side in New York. The way I like to remember is that Abraham-Hicks' book, *The Essential Law of Attraction Collection*, magically fell into my hands.

I was mesmerized by this book so much that I stopped reading everything else for a very long time. After gently sharing with Kosta the impact I was experiencing from reading this book, he eventually gave in himself and started reading it, too. We ended up buying many copies and giving them to family, friends, and people in the streets of New York. *The Essential Law of Attraction Collection* had all the questions and answers I had ever wanted to know at that time.

We had been applying the teaching of Abraham-Hicks for three years before we joined the first Abraham cruise-workshop, where we made many lifelong friends. Many of them were noticing how steady, calm, and easy Kosta was, so I began to joke with him saying, "When will you start channeling?"

Two years later, just a week after arriving from another 2020 Abraham-Hicks Caribbean cruise, Kosta noticed a flow of thoughts that felt different during his morning meditation. He decided to record himself, and to our surprise, the words that came out were in Serbian, his native language, despite the fact that for years he had been used to thinking and expressing himself in English.

Looking back, Kosta shared with me that he realized it was not the first time he had felt steady thoughts flowing through his being during a meditation. However, it was the first time he had become aware of what was happening and had chosen to document it.

Since then, Kosta and I would sit every morning in our patio and read together the wisdom received through the flow. My excitement to share it with everyone led me to invite a few close friends to experience a session of the newly discovered receiving, where Kosta let answers to any questions asked by others flow through Weola.

Gradually but fast, Weola sessions became consistent weekly broadcasts with a variety of people, many of whom are inspirational facilitators, life coaches and uplifters even today. In just two years, we created 9 intuitive programs, hosted more than 100+ livestreams and 9 in-person retreats, created Look Within Magazine and Look Within Branding.

It is hard to put in words the unfolding of the impact and difference we are continually making. I will let you discover that for yourself by reading this book.

There is one thing that I am very intentional and clear about. I want you to recognize your wholeness within yourself. This will not be the only book or the only tool to do so—but it is certainly a powerful one.

Whether this is a starting point in your spiritual journey, or you have been around the block for some time, this material will bring you a new, valuable clarity in your never-ending self-discovery movement.

Enjoy the dance!

WEOLA'S FIRST WORDS

"Here, now, present in your desire to be constantly connected. And to express the Wider Perspective this way, and to express it to others, too. For now, this way seems the simplest one because it is your native language. So, there is no confusion that the words that are used are authentically yours.

This way of receiving probably suits you the most for now. It is ok to take this feeling and stabilize it so you can get used to it—easy to this whole flow that is going on. To your focusing mechanism that functions as a receiver of all messages, for you to use whenever it suits you.

And anytime you want, with identical conditions like now, many are here, together, focused now, wherever you are, ready to pave the way for the development of the next step for every question you have.

Here, ready whenever you or someone else has a question. Easy, easy with joy, easy.

And for now, this is it."

THE QUESTION-ANSWER DANCE

Since then, Kosta would meditate every morning, tuning into the Wider Perspective, and we would joyously interact, me asking questions and Kosta flowing the answers. That became the most exciting part of the day for us. It was beautiful to observe us both shifting, where each of us was getting comfortable with this steadiness of the energy flow, each in our own way.

As Kosta and I were adjusting to this new experience, we received the following words:

"This is Your width, your length, your full, complete, total, overall being, together with you. Here, ready for any question that will come in the future, and for now as an announcement.

So Kosta, in his own way, builds continuity in receiving answers that will be arriving with various questions. For this process, there is a necessity for a little bit of practice, and with time, it will come with more simplicity and in different forms. Here and now, ready to allow Kosta to get used to this flow of information slowly, simply, step by step—to the information that is available to everyone in every given moment. For all that have an open channel, a tuned in receiver.

Specific information for what people are ready to hear, for anyone who asks a question in this format. Receiving this knowledge and this information that comes across this way is the next natural step for the ones in the vicinity of being aware of their own authentic connection.

This is a new way for Kosta to express, by uninterrupted flow in real-time, the one he has desired in a crisp form like this since he was born. No judgment, sincere perspective that is coming from the source of Everything That Exists.

Practice is everything. Where there is a desire for something, practice gets set up as the next step. Now is the path for enjoyment and arrival of information, at the time when that specific information is for the benefit of the one who is listening.

And for now, this is it."

WHAT IS YOUR NAME

Many, including us, often referred to "channeling" as something "woo woo." Now, we have a clear knowing that with no exception, everyone is connected to that which many call God, Source, Divine, Universe, or The Essence of Everything That Exists.

We all dance between our Wider Perspective and Self-Perspective at all times.

Kosta developed the skill to be more consistent in meditative state, something that anyone can accomplish with practice. In that state, personal thoughts, opinions, and beliefs are so soft that they don't interfere with the flow that is not habitual, but comes from our God-like perspective.

After about six weeks of interacting with each other, during an intimate online gathering with friends who were curious about Kosta's steady energy flow, we noticed that people wanted to know how to refer to Kosta while in the session. So I asked: "I want to take this message that I want to slowly share with a circle of people, and it is an expectation that anyone who has access to the source of Everything That Exists in this way also has some type of name. So, I wonder whether the name is needed, and if so, what is your name?"

WE ALL ARE ONE

The answer followed swiftly and, as you will read, it was longer than before, which became increasingly the norm due to Kosta's comfort and steadiness.

"In every focusing mechanism, there is either awareness or lack of awareness of the presence of the Wider Perspective from moment to moment. Only a mechanism that can focus can observe the presence and absence of it. There are also differences in the Wider Perspective, but they are so subtle that they never cause trouble.

The physical environment has so much variety and variation in its expression, that it is inevitable that it focuses much more on what is the absence of expression and a life of coincidence with the Wider Perspective.

Different people, who find consistency in being One with the source of Everything That Exists in a seamless and real-time way, are translating what everyone has access to.

A name appointment, as Kosta well knows, is needed by some people for expression, that is, for connection. Some people, especially those who are just becoming aware of this, need Wider Perspective to have some form, some kind of name, in order to have a familiar style of conversation, because the person being "interviewed" is a person with access to this kind of unhindered communication.

There is no desire to express in this way because Kosta's clarity on Everything That Exists is that everyone has access to this, and that any conversation that will proceed while Kosta's channel is open will put them in a position of unhindered receiving of answers, even though they don't flow them directly at that moment.

Individual expressions are fascinating; individual expressions through larger and larger numbers of people. The process that happens almost daily now for Kosta is only the beginning of what will bring interactions with many other people. They will be able to witness the value of the process that happens, and find more and more such moments on their own.

It is interesting to see how his clear knowing began to be influenced by some situations regarding the spread of this message through his receiving mechanism. It is a completely natural consequence and an experience of every focusing mechanism. Comparing, comparing, comparing with others for validation reasons, for confirming that a passing message will be accepted or not by people who are used to it or not.

The flow coming through Kosta's receiving mechanism will reach the exact people who need it at the moment. And to them, the understanding of all that is happening will be so clear that the name will not be important to them, as it is not to Kosta.

All the moments that give evidence and confirm the well-being nature of Everything That Exists are important moments that contribute to the flow of wholeness and bring every focusing mechanism to become even firmer, steadier and positive in their choices.

We All Are One.

And for now, with great satisfaction in the awareness that We All Are One.

Maybe that is the best way to describe us.

And for now, that's it."

That was an exciting message for us, after which Kosta, playing with the words, received a shorter version, a nickname derived from We All Are One – WEOLA. "Ola" in Spanish means "wave." So, it can also be read as "We All Are One Wave."

As you will discover soon, Weola talks about the eternal movement of Everything That Exists, at all times.

SATURDAY, JULY 24TH, 2021, 11:11 AM, BELGRADE, SERBIA.

WEOLA'S OPENNING

Here, now, present at this moment, at every moment, at all times. Your Wider Perspective, a different dimension, that which is non-physical, always accessible to you as there is no separation between a physical, uniquely focused aspect of you, and that which is the Wider Perspective.

So much thrill has been coming through in this beautiful dance Kosta and Armand have been having since the original receiving of this flow. So many answers have been seen and realized by those who have been asking questions. And now, it is time for that experience to be broadened and available in a format of a written word, too.

And so, as you get to read the upcoming pages, be easy with the process. Easy to receive everything that is, at this moment, available to you. For you to experience this as the starting point for many more in-depth questions, as they arrive in the future during reflections like these.

This content has been percolating, shaping up, and it has taken the form applicable for this moment in time.

We will start with the flow of each session and then allow for as many questions as you have. We will go as detailed as possible in each of these segments, and allow the questions to take the reflection further.

Enjoy the ride!

CHAPTER ONE
WHO YOU ARE

THE PERSPECTIVE OF SELF

What you are observing in your surroundings is available to you through the awareness of your physical vessel that is sensing everything around you. The physicality of you, the physicality of others, the physicality of the planet, the tangibility of it all. Everything experienced through your physical senses is constantly stimulating you to be present in the place of *focus*.

That which you observe around you is an accumulation of everything that has been before this very moment, and it continues to evolve and to be more, with every now that becomes before, and every future moment that becomes now, and then becomes before. And so, it is safe to say that you are an accumulation of Everything That Exists, that has been embodied in physicality, either by you or by everything and everyone before you. You are that physical accumulation, that evolved accumulation of all knowledge.

You are that singular organism that developed into a multiple-cell life form that kept developing into more and that is now this highly orchestrated mechanism that you are experiencing it to be. Therefore, within you, there is an immense amount of physical focus embodied, transferred from one generation to another by observing, interacting and sharing, but also by your experience of coming through to this and every other physical iteration.

Your engaging focused experience sometimes gets you to feel as if it is all there is to encounter. However, as you came from the perspective of physical *unfocus*, and got into this, focused form unique to you, this is just the current state of your experience.

If you observe how babies turn into kids, kids turn into young adults, young adults turn into adults, you can witness that the amount of focus is gradually moving from a lot of unfocused time and not being able to keep attention, to more of the attention coming into the focal point. Sometimes, through the stimulation of your physicality, you get to have a lot of emphasis on your attention outwards, and that creates a lot of sharpness in your focus through your physical senses. And therefore, for a moment, it might not be on your radar that there are dimensions to you other than your physical aspect.

By living like this, you might reach an overstimulated point filled with so much focus that in not being able to hold it any longer, you allow yourself to experience something else. To discover this *Wider Perspective*, from which the words you are now reading are coming. Sometimes, it is not until the end of your physical iteration, and at other times it is rather early that you realize there is more to you. Then you get to consistently keep this *awareness* throughout the rest of your life.

It might also be that you are among the ones who came to physicality and have been experiencing a more balanced flow of life expression. You have commenced from the same pure, unfocused embodiment and took form in physicality, and got to gradually build the focusing muscle, without having it be the only one active for the majority of time.

Regardless of what got you here, how you are living now or what you choose to live in the future, all your experiences are valuable for you in your eternal journey.

The boundedness of your physicality is that which you are experiencing to be the physical form. The shape of you, compared to the shape of someone else, compared to the shape of a tree, an animal, cloud, to the shape of the building, of every living and inanimate object. As you are so focused in your physical senses, and as the accumulation of all the generations before is still so present within you, it is understandable why sometimes it is tricky to sense that there is more than just the dimension of separateness.

This is your **perspective of Self**. The perspective of your unique vantage point from which Everything That Exists, embodied in you, is expressed through your experiences and the process of experiencing. This perspective is so beneficial to you and everyone around you, as it provides the unique points, the unique angles from which your questions are being born. Everyone has their own lens to gather details unique to that moment. And then, based on the collected input, you get to discover the answers that become available not only to you, but to everyone else looking to experience a similar or same topic in their own journey.

As this conversation about other dimensions of your experience goes on, you will see how beneficial and how important your physical focus and your perspective is, and how that uniqueness keeps propelling the eternal movement of Everything That Exists. *You will also grasp that it is not the only perspective you have.* To be easy about discovering the chapters ahead is to find the resonance with the process of discovery. Not only about identifying that there is a different perspective, but also how to get to that perspective any time you desire, and use it as a fuel for empowerment of your own physical experience. Knowing that everything that you are creating and experiencing in your physicality is the work of you, integrated and balanced in eternal dance between your physical and the Wider Perspectives.

You mentioned before that as we ask the questions, all the answers are simultaneously created. Where, how, and why is this information (answers) being stored?

There is an infinite amount of information available to you and everyone else and yet, there is no physical entity where you upload your thoughts and where they are being stored. Everything that has ever been asked and answered is flowing, floating around, so you can think of it as a consistent, *eternal movement*. Based on where you are oscillating at the moment – you are checking in, or you are catching, you are matching yourself up with one or a variety of states of being that you are moving through and therefore receiving. You are doing this either to ask those questions or to receive the answers. *This whole process is at all times within you.* All of the answers you receive are at all times within you as the questions are being born. And so there is no physical place for you to go to, there is no particular storage to which you need access. All of your experience is always within you.

How do we come into physicality? Why do some come more in balance and others unbalanced? And what does balance mean?

The continuity between your physical iterations is always based on what you do within each and every one of them. In other words, there is no experience such as regression, where you might be experiencing one kind of work that you do, or things that you know, or the balances that you are making, and then coming back again to square one. The freshness of the new point between your physical iterations is, at all times, only serving you to continue the flow of your evolution.

And so, what you observe as someone being more in balance, compared to some other being more unbalanced, is just that someone has been finding more of this integrated experience and consciously applying the Wider Perspective in their experience of physicality. There are also many being suspicious about physicality being nothing more than that. In such a variety of experiences, what you are getting from each and other physical iteration is a new perspective for you to express more of your Wider Perspective. For you to continue your eternal quest to fully experience more and more of *your entire human potential*, that spans and encompasses so much more than just surviving by using physical focus. Your physical body vessel, your mind, and your emotions are the tools that you are gathering and that you can be using in each and every physical iteration for your life experience to be way more than just figuring out where to find shelter, what to eat and how to nourish yourself in that basic way.

Some of your faculties tend to be more overused, and therefore bring you to a place of less balance. This Wider Perspective of you is not something that you get and reach, it is not something you need to plug yourself into. It is such a big part of you, such a strong part of you, such an overwhelmingly dominant part of you, that it is constantly there for you to check in, so you can perceive from that perspective more often and find that which you call balance. This balancing game is realizing that the form of physicality is not the only aspect of you that is active in your life experience.

There is no focusing mechanism, especially human focusing mechanism, that has not, at some point, thought or asked questions about being more than physical being. Some more often, some not as much, but everyone at one point finds themselves asking: "Is there more to me, and if there is, what is it? Who am I and what am I experiencing day in and day out? Is that all there is – my physical body and my mind experiencing my own mix of thoughts and emotions?"

Sometimes, the focus is bringing so much consumption of information that your attention does not move with ease to other directions. That is why so many people experience that state of not having balance.

Your life experience is an individual quest based on the Wider Perspective you embody. Therefore, all of the answers are always within you. And all the tools you discover along the way to get in the vicinity of balance and experience predominantly from the state of Wider Perspective are for you, so you can apply them to all of your thrilling physical activities.

Why do we come to physicality?

For the joy of being expressed. For the experience of finding more and more balance. Because from the perspective of variety that you are observing, so many questions are arising and new balances are being born. To look for more ways to express, then explore, then express again. And when the new balances are being found, you get to experience new layers of that which is a Wider Perspective. Which brings you to experience the fullness of your human potential reflected in the state of bliss so many are talking about.

You come to observe the variety, ask questions, get the physical understanding of it, and then move to the discovery process of realizing those answers. And from that point, to apply your satisfaction with the received answer and fly into the new curiosity.

You cannot have enough of that which is physical experience, because you are consistently looking for more of you to be expressed. That is how and why Everything That Exists constantly expands and that feeling of expansion can be experienced so thrillingly from each and one of the infinite perspectives of Self.

What is the difference between humans and the rest of the physical world like animals, nature, and everything around us?

You once were that animal, you once were that plant, you once were that single organism you are observing. Your choices brought to you your evolution, that took you to the place where you can further experience so much more than before. Because of the expansion and the evolutionary jump that you made, that your ancestors had made, and that you continue to make with everything that you are giving your attention to. The brilliance of the complexity of your system is so subtle and so perfect in its own way, but it requires balanced activity in order for you to realize more into your experience than mere survival.

When you are consistently and predominantly focused outwards, almost anything to which you give your attention can light up a survival mode within you. At those moments, you are putting an equal sign between you and all the other beings you see around. On the other hand, when you are not stimulated by variety, you can access and explore more sophisticated dimensions of expressing life. For as long as you get to the state of real exploration, you have, at that moment, more potential than any other being on the planet to unlock infinite possibilities within you.

And so, it is not that other beings are not joyful. It is not that they are not having their experience of the Wider Perspective. It is not that they are not continuously emerging and expanding as well. But you have gotten through that phase, and now you are in a perspective where you can explore a variety of different dimensions, such as producing long term beneficial conclusions. But also moving yourself from the long effects of those conclusions by satisfying your survival needs and moving onto finding tools that give you a quiet and balanced mind.

Even when you observe the times that you are in, you can see that there is not much that is necessary for you to be in a place of safety. For a big part of the population, there is an ease in providing shelter and basic necessities. Everything else you give your attention to and that you choose to desire does not have to be approached from that place of necessity. Having this awareness is really what makes a different experience for you than any other beautiful being coming through and looking to balance out its predominantly surviving experience.

That, which is your awareness of being separate from others is the starting point in your evolution. As you experience more variety, you get to ask questions about being more than that. When your basic needs are satisfied, you are ready to experience more. And that which you are looking to experience more of is always within you. It is the Wider Perspective of One.

THE PERSPECTIVE OF ONE

Everything is One.

You can experience this perspective the moment you get to practice a little bit of unfocusing, a quiet mind, the sense of not being so active in your actions. From a Wider Perspective you can perceive that there is no difference between you and anything to which you give your attention. That everything is really you from a different angle.

As you get to practice softening your thoughts, you are on the way to really grasp and fully experience the Wider Perspective. *Everything you give your attention to is a reflection of you, back to you.* The Wider Perspective embodied by you and everyone else in that perspective of Self while measuring, and comparing, and noticing, and observing, and choosing, and making decisions based on all that physical action. *But in essence, One.* The breath you take was someone else's exhalation. Your exhalation becomes someone else's inhalation, and so, everything is at all times interconnected.

This Wider Perspective is not a destination. It is not a location for you to get to. It is part of every particle there is. Therefore, it is part of all of you at all times, making up for the majority of which you are – a unique physical vessel, holding a Wider Perspective for the time of this and every iteration.

And so as you look within, even once in a while, you come to notice this interconnectedness. You comprehend the Oneness we are talking about. You witness that Everything That Exists has variety – infinite, physical vantage points and angles from which it can be perceived. And while there are individual decisions being made from the point of Self, that which is the reflection that comes to you, based on anything that you are observing or interacting with, is you from a different angle.

> ***I'm curious. Could you help us and deepen your explanation of what you mean by "me from a different angle?" What is this about and how does this apply to our life experiences?***

If you could imagine yourself being in the ocean, and capturing, with both of your hands together, a certain amount of water. And then as you move through the water, still holding the hands together, they capture other particles of water, too. This analogy is for you to notice how your physicality captures different aspects of Everything That Exists at different times, as you have access to each and every other droplet in the infinitely evolving interconnected ocean of your Wider Perspective.

You can see yourself separate from others, which happens when you are predominantly focused. You can also soften up your focus and start viewing others as a reflection of you. And then you can go even further in your dance between the focus and unfocus and get to the place where you see that you are One with everything, and therefore everyone represents a different angle of you.

Most of the time, this different angle of you assists you in generating the questions, but it is also there for you to hear something that you do not hear while looking within. In other words, to point back to you a different avenue of discovery, so you receive that which you have not received before.

When you get to find more balance between the amount of focus that is going outwards and the frequency of unfocusing as often as you can, you get to experience things, people and situations as not separate from you. Then you see that everyone, in a way, is talking to you, that everything that you are observing can be of benefit to you. You see that everything that you are and everyone you are interacting with has value to you. And once you grasp that, then you fully understand that it is all you. You from a different angle, providing that value to yourself.

This does not mean that you get to control others, nor do you get to have anyone do what you want them to do. But based on what you observe, you get to choose what you make out of the variety and how valuable you perceive it at that moment. Because all of it has an infinite value for you.

> ***How exactly does this reflection work? I would like an analogy for more clarity, because people may be making other people uncomfortable with their actions. How and why does this happen? Why is there a value in it and how can we apply that value and benefit from it?***

When you are mostly focused, and giving attention outwards, you are observing from the perspective of Self. When you see yourself as different from others, you might believe that someone is doing something to you. That becomes apparent even more when someone is trying to do something negative to you. Then it might be even more difficult to see why there would be any value in that.

Try to imagine that there is no other reflection but satisfaction coming to you. Everything that you are observing is positive in nature. And therefore, all that you are getting is simply satisfying. Keep imagining that anything that you are observing is not bringing you any questions. Everything that you are observing is not triggering within you the quest to see things from a different perspective. It is possible for this to become your predominant experience, but only when you realize that there is no difference between you and the others.

When you are experiencing others as different, it represents the beginning of discovery for you. You might be there predominantly at this time, but you do not have to be there predominantly at all times. When you get to the state of softening up your attention given outwards, you start pulling into the Wider Perspective. This is the start of seeing the benefits which reflections bring to you, either to formulate your desire, or to reflect back to you the evidence that what you desired before is now showing up in your reality.

Once you understand that everything you give your attention to is a *mirror reflection,* then you start noticing where you are in your own discovery of question-answer dance or focus-unfocus dance. So you get to that state of witnessing that everything reflecting back to you has value in your eternal development game.

You are not in physicality to experience elimination of the questions, because removing questions would eliminate the desires. And not having desires would put a stop to eternity, which cannot be. You are looking to be in balance so much so that asking questions becomes a thrill of curiosity, rather than a burden. When you find yourself dominant in your focus, the moment you satisfy your basic needs, you are ready to shift into discovery of that which is a Wider Perspective.

Once that movement commences, once your attention is not predominantly outwards to compare and measure yourself to other Selves, but moves into a Wider Perspective more often, you set in motion the process of blurring the lines, and start experiencing the Oneness of it all. You then know the benefit of someone who appears to be coming at you or doing something to you. It simply represents the starting point in your discovery.

From your perspective of Self, comparing to the others from their perspective of Self is at all times providing you with feedback, a reflection of where you are at the moment so you can choose where to continue the movement to next.

You talk about the balance and then quieting your mind? Why does breathing bring balance? And what do you mean by saying that all answers can be accessed by going within?

From this Wider Perspective, you come into physicality expressing yourself through your body, through your mind, through your emotions into your physical life energies. *But you are not the body, the mind, nor your thoughts or emotions.*

The body is yours, the mind is yours, the emotions are yours, and the thoughts are yours, but it is not you. You are this Wider Perspective, this Everything That Exists perspective, expressing yourself through all of these wonderful faculties.

When you soften up your body so it is not sensing stimulation too much, when you soften up your mind so it is not processing too much, when you soften up your emotions, so they are not triggering within you too much – you allow your physical energies to be balanced. The breathwork is one of the key components to get there, as it is one of the few automatic processes in your body you can easily control.

Many things within your physicality you are not in charge of; how your brain is working, or how your neurons are working, or how your blood is going through. You are not consciously digesting the food, you are not consciously renewing your skin, you are not consciously doing any of that. You can have a more conscious experience of these functions, but you are not really in need to do any of that because it is perfectly orchestrated and your body is automatically and consistently looking for balance.

What you can get to experience more of is the quieting of your physicality. Not only your mind, but all physical senses, so thoughts and emotions soften up and you become alert and receptive to different dimensions, to different perspectives, to different angles of your experience.

Allowing yourself to become predominantly one with your breath allows you to start blurring the lines of that which is laser sharp focus, and gets you to the state where you can experience from a Wider Perspective, from a vantage point of more inclusion, from the perspective of One.

That is why breathing is often referred to as a gateway to other dimensions of life experience.

> ***You also mentioned before that we are not energies, that the energies are ours. And I had the perception that energy is actually the Wider Perspective, meaning that energy is the Source and everything and everyone around us is energy. So for me, this is new. And I would like to have more clarity on what you mean by saying that we are not the energies? I feel I am still caught up with the idea that we are vibration and that we are energy. And that we are just translating that energy and that vibration into physicality. So, isn't that a Wider Perspective? Isn't it simply the energy?***

Your physical sense and evidence of energy that you are embodying within you is another tool for you to check your balance between your focus and unfocus, or question and answer, or that which is the perspective of Self and the One. In other words, the physicality of your energy goes up or down based on your sense of how balanced you are.

It is the eternal movement between the question and the answer, between the focus and unfocus that gets this which you call vibration or oscillation to happen. The movement is what keeps, at all times, that which you call creation or experience of the energy that you can sense through your physicality.

There is not this one plug that everything is coming from. The movement is what keeps creation going. The movement between each question that is being asked, and each answer that is being received, while expanding that which you might refer to as the grid of Everything That Exists.

Probably the closest way for you to describe the movement between the non-physical and the physical is through the way of energy. But we want to make sure you understand that what you feel as the energy within your body also varies based on your balance between how much attention you give to physical stimulation, and how frequently you withdraw your attention from it.

> ***So how does this movement happen? What does movement mean, and what or who moves?***

You, and every other focusing mechanism with every question that is being asked in infinite amounts, moment in and moment out. Consistency of movement is based on a reflection. When you consistently observe what is happening within you, and what is happening around you, you are provided with consistent feedback. More feedback keeps coming with everything you give attention to. And based on that, there is consistent movement in your attention going somewhere, and then reflecting back to you, going somewhere and then coming back to you, going somewhere and then rebounding back to you. *And like that, you keep moving for all eternity.*

AN INTEGRATED ONE-SELF EXPERIENCE

There is no separation between that which is your physical perspective, and that which is your Wider Perspective. Or that which is within you, and that which is experienced on a perimeter of you as you explore.

Everything That Exists makes up for 99.99999% of it all. If you look into the physicality of the structure of the physical matter, on atom and cell levels, you will see that there is mostly this invisible space covered, shaped within movement of electrons, protons and neutrons. All of that which you might call empty space, and many call ether or intangible space—all of that is within every single particle of the Universe, and therefore within every single part of you, within every single cell that you contain at this and in any other moment. And it is all consistently in motion.

That is why we say that a Wider Perspective is consistently within you and there is nothing that you need to connect to, because every single particle of you is made out of it. It is about your awareness of where your *attention* is going at different times, in order for you to fully experience your integrated life experience.

When your attention is predominantly in your physicality, in a perspective of Self, you are not very much aware of One. You see yourself as separate from others, you are comparing, you might be feeling that you are you, and someone else is them, and that you are doing things to each other. When you quiet your physical senses for a moment, then you start becoming receptive to different dimensions of your experience, and that is the time when you start seeing how integrated with everything and everyone you are.

It is not about reaching a Wider Perspective and diminishing your physicality, as while you are still in your vessel, you cannot have that. Even the ones that are meditating the most, those masters that you might be hearing about, or whose work you might be witnessing – they keep using a variety of tools consistently to stay within the dimension of focus, while experiencing a Wider Perspective. Integration is always present at all times. And so, you are not in this experience to try to get yourself to a Wider Perspective and try to stay there by holding on to it. *You are here to experience the awareness of all the dimensions of life.* And then enjoy the glorious blendedness of them all.

You are here to mostly be aware of your physicality. Then, occasionally, check in with and enjoy Everything That Exists fully and apply that awareness to everything you do from a perspective of Self— gather some more variety, observe while collecting data and information, get your curiosities, and then release them so you can go back to experience those answers as you are back in the unfocusing part of the process.

This integrated blended experience is what you are at all times. As you move from that perspective of focus, and you experience the process of unfocusing, you are then able to see this experience of your physicality from a more integrated position, while firmly holding the reins of all aspects of your own creation process.

Interconnectedness. Integration. Inclusiveness.

That is what you are all about.

What is the purpose of the Self and the One?

No other purpose. No other but exploration and discovery of how many more expressions of that which you are can find showing in your physicality. There is nothing that you need to do or have to do. On a daily basis, many situations might show up and activate within you the feeling of necessity or need. But you really need very little to sustain your physical experience, so everything beyond that can be an exploration of different dimensions of life.

You are this life force expressing through the tools of physicality – your mind, your body, thoughts and emotions. You are here to have that current experience, which is now, now, now. As you become aware of a Wider Perspective, you can have the whole Universe, the whole Cosmos being experienced by you, because it is all within you, at all times.

So, how would you describe life? What is life?

Life is a dance between question and answer. Life is the force within you, looking to express itself. Your physical body, mind, thoughts and emotions are not making for all of your life. They are the vessels in which your life is finding the expression. You are never really just that body, or just that mind, or just that emotion that you are experiencing. You are so much more than that. You are this Divine, God, Source, Everything That Exists perspective, experiencing so much variety, integrating that into eternity and bringing it more into variety, perpetually and forever more.

Curiosity leads to discovery; curiosity brings feedback for you to discover more from it. To be more curious, so you can discover more. To be more curious on the outskirts of you, so you can discover more within you. So you can be more curious while giving attention outward, and so you can discover more by going within.

This dance makes for the pulse of Everything That Exists.

Before you mentioned that you are trying to stay away from the word "manifestation" or "manifest" on purpose while speaking that there is no purpose. Why is that?

This word often causes necessity to prove its showing in reality as the ultimate goal. Those goals and those desires that you have are just the beginning part of your discovery. And you are in it for all the discovery, not only for the moment of witnessing that which is showing or manifesting in your experience.

Sometimes that word can be a good starting point to move you from your attention in physicality only, from giving your attention to so many questions. To move you from the direction of curiosity turning into questions, then into problems and into a lot of discomfort, and shift you to the place of knowing that there is something else as an option to experience. For once your question is hatched, once you know how everything operates and that you are at the head of it all, and at all times, life becomes only about the practice of ease.

That which you call manifestation is proof of what once was your curiosity that is now showing up. It is only one tiny part of this wonderful experience, where you can have infinite moments of satisfaction coming through you. Not only to open that one gift box at the end in the form of manifestation, but infinite gift boxes in a process of discovering that which is manifestation.

Oftentimes, because you get so good at discovering and seeing those little gift boxes along the way, the gift box that you opened up at the end does not really seem as important as realizing how satisfying the whole discovery process was. It is not that there is no satisfaction in manifestation, but sometimes that particular word can keep you away from getting to it sooner and enjoying every segment of the discovery along the way.

> ***I went through being aware that there is more than just the physicality I observe, to recognizing that there is a Wider Perspective, often referred to as the Universe or Source. Yet, I was still seeing myself as separate from it, even embracing statements such as "the Universe has my back." Now I understand that it is me having my own back. Which makes me curious if there is a statement or your reflection on the analogy of that saying?***

At all times, you are on the cusp of realizing what is fully your nature. *It is really available to everyone, at all times, to experience.* Those who are so physically focused, and not really trusting that there is anything more, seeing themselves separate from others and in a place of predominantly asking questions - they, as the next step for them, get to hear intellectually first, and then eventually feel – that there is more to them. Usually it shows as someone holding the feel good space for them, holding the steadiness for them so they can start moving in a direction of experiencing more than physicality.

For most people, the first step is – *"I'm just physical and I do not see anything else but that."* That is followed by – *"I see that there is more than the physical part of me but I feel separateness from it."*

Since there is too much focus still in the dimension of physicality, the consistency of the movement between perspectives is not established enough. In other words, the process of unfocusing from the physicality to experience a Wider Perspective is not there with consistency. Therefore, they see that there is more than physicality to them, but they still see themselves separate from it.

You witness how many see themselves different from a God in any religion, they see themselves being one way and God being the other way. And then you see a lot of spiritual people using a substitute for that which used to be religion. It is still something on the "other side," even though more positive, even though less judgmental. When you seek for more, you start experiencing, so clearly and so steadily, that both of the perspectives are accessible to you at all times, and that it is time for you to move to the next layer of view, *which does not see differences.*

You are not creating the tree next to you, you are not having the whole planet spin around on its own, you are not the one doing that. But you are participating in that, within the reach of your own reflection. As you keep having experiences of being so physical, and then allowing yourself to be soft and gradually experience a Wider Perspective, you see that it is like making a new friend. You first simply shake the hand, you do not go and give immediately all of the unbounded access to you. You test it out a little bit, you see a Wider Perspective as different. You talk to it as if it is your best friend, as if it is someone who is cheering for you, someone who has your back.

Until you realize it has all been you, at all times.

When you get to see yourself from the perspective of Self, while being aware that separateness between physical and non-physical does not exist, everything around you starts becoming a *reflection*. And that reflection can turn into *all-inclusiveness*, given your desire for a consistency in finding the balance while giving attention to anything. When you activate the perspective of softer thought more often, you allow yourself to experience more of Oneness.

Great! From here, what would be the next logical topic to reflect on?

There is more to you than your physical focus. There is a Wider Perspective of you, integrated with the physical aspect of you.

You are the perspective of One embodied in your physical Self, while using your physical body, mind, your thoughts and emotions as tools for your expression.

This is a starting point that will allow you to open yourself up to the possibility of living a full human experience.

CHAPTER TWO

THE BALANCE

THE CREATION PROCESS

As you commence experiencing your physicality by observing variety, and start noticing the cause and effect, you start witnessing how certain things influence other things, how certain situations affect other situations in a form of patterns, and you start drawing conclusions.

However, there is nothing really to conclude in anything which you are experiencing.

All of your thoughts, opinions, beliefs, judgments, and matching emotions being experienced are tools for you to express. In your attention outwards, they are the starting point of your discovery. They are a revelation of a Wider Perspective embodied, and then the application of that awareness into anything and everything you give attention to.

You are a human being, but you are also being a God. You are that Divine flow that is having experience within the body, and therefore, all the answers that you are ever looking for are within. When we say God, we mean *an active participant in putting forward everything that you observe* as your reality. Participant, not only a spectator. As you start being more aware of both of your roles as a spectator and as a participant in your creation, you also see that you are that creation itself, too.

You are the creation, and you are creating, and you are the creator.

While the roles that you are playing are integrated and happening at once, they are not active within your attention simultaneously, so you play them one at a time. This makes it easier for you to organize and practice your muscle of attention in a direction that will bring you a more satisfying ride, a more blissful experience in your mind and body, as your thoughts and emotions continue to keep becoming a legacy of your choice.

You observe and make choices. You are observing, and making choices. You are always observing, and based on what you perceive, you are always making choices. When you consciously make a choice in a direction that interests you, you receive the clarity of your wanting, and now you are on the wave of that wanting. So, you are observing and choosing, observing and choosing, observing and choosing and when you get the clarity of wanting you set the trajectory of experiencing it. But it is not until you *release your attention from wanting*, that you start unveiling the ways that get you to experience the reality of that desire.

You observe and choose to get the clarity and catch the wave of your wanting sufficiently to take your attention away from the action of observing and choosing for some time. When you are unclouded about that which is your precise wanting, you do not continue to spend time looking around and measuring up, because you have the clarity of your current wanting.

How long you keep your attention in the wanting depends on how strong of a wanting it is, and how long it took you to get to it. When it is about a topic which is not so important, you release it rather quickly. If it took you some time to clarify it, you tend to give it more attention. And sometimes, by giving more attention to it, you introduce the awareness of the gap between what you want and when you are to experience it.

The suggestion is that once you get the clarity of the wanting, you release it.

You release your attention from your wanting, and give your attention to other topics that bring you to be present in the moment, so you move into the beauty of discovery. For as you shift the attention away from the clarity of wanting, you also shift the attention from the observing-choosing part altogether, from the measuring up part of the creation process. You shift away from giving attention to that which has hatched as an idea, as a desire, as the clarity of wanting, and by doing that you point it out to a possibility of its experience in your physical reality.

You can go about it like this.

Observe and choose, observe and choose, observe and choose. Sometimes more, sometimes less, depending on the topic that puts the observing into the motion. Get the clarity of wanting and catch the wave of it. Now it is transparent to you what you want, therefore – release it, so it shows itself to you. Release it, so you can notice the possibility that lights up, the most satisfying one among infinite possibilities of discovery. All while observing and choosing and hatching new clarities of new wants along the way.

It is in the release of desire that your real discovery begins. That is when all of the "hows" and "whens" are unveiled to you, all of the "whys" start showing up to you. Therefore, you do not need to try to program and project them, because you have released attention from both the observe-choose and clarity of the wanting part of the process. And now it is all about the satisfaction of discovery.

THE CREATION PROCESS. VISUAL 1.

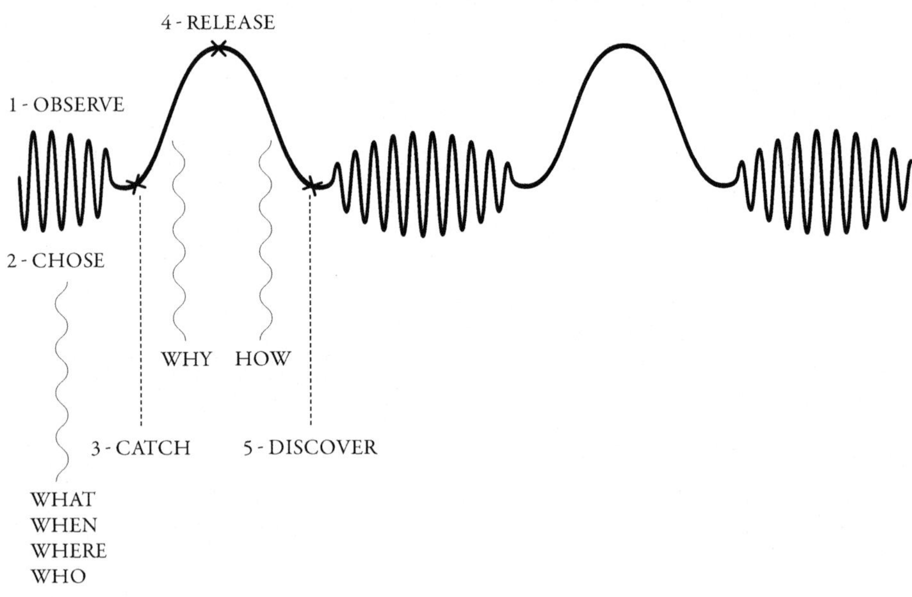

1 - OBSERVE the variety
2 - CHOOSE from variety
3 - CATCH the wave of wanting
4 - RELEASE the clarity of wanting
5 - DISCOVER in physicality what you once wanted

While you are in a process of discovering the desire in reality on one topic, you have the observe-choose experiences for many others. While you are on the way to discover that specific gift box, which you have put together by clarifying your wanting, you have an opportunity for more than going back and revisiting the same wanting again and again until you finally see it. Even though that is possible, even though you can zone in on that one wanting, you can also joyfully be present in the moment and be in the process of forming, orchestrating and realizing the delivery of so many more gift boxes along the way.

When you release the wanting of what you consider to be the bigger desire, you realize that there are so many others to be discovered along the way. So many more gift boxes, even though representing smaller and less significant desires, are available to be opened by you, and to bring you confidence along the way. Those are the ones that show you the evidence of all the aspects of the creation process. The ones that demonstrate the possibilities of experiencing with ease, because you did not think about them non-stop on the way to receive them.

Therefore, the suggestion is to go for releasing your wanting and not to force a decision in which order you are to open up your gift boxes, in which order they are to show up to you. As it is not the order that you are looking to grasp, but the infinite possibilities of satisfaction and bliss in the next moment, of the next circumstance, and the next situation. Releasing the clarity of the wanting into discovery is what *being present in the now* means. It means simply *being and experiencing*. And therefore, even desires and their fulfillment, while satisfying, become miniscule compared to the bliss brought to you by the process of conscious discovery.

When you experience the now, you realize who you actually are. You understand *you are the process*. Inevitable, eternal, perpetual *process of discovery*.

Can you describe in a little bit more detail what it means to observe variety?

Anything that you give your conscious attention to, or anything that you pick up with your senses of physicality spontaneously. When you give attention through your mind, or when your physical body is picking up through its receptors, all around you, all of it contains a variety you are constantly scanning. Everything that is outwardly focused from you is an observation of variety.

You open your eyes, and you observe with them. You hear the sound and you observe with your ears. You smell the food, and you observe with your nose. Everything that you are observing either through your imagination or through your physical observation of what you call reality or facts, or "what is" – all of it makes up for variety.

The way you perceive variety is never perceived by anyone else in the same way. And what you perceive now will never be perceived by you in the same way, the way it is in that moment, again. What you are perceiving and observing outwards is constantly changing, and you are consistently having the new opportunities for new perspectives. And so does every other focusing mechanism.

That which you observe as separate from you is your perspective of Self looking at someone or something in their perspective of Self. You observe the shapes, movements, differences, varieties and all of that radiant feedback that you are getting is based on that which is not the same. That process of such brilliant, cohesive movement of differences is from where you get to commence all of your discoveries.

> ***So, variety can also be observed in thoughts? Meaning, if I close my eyes, and I imagine something, whatever it is, it is also observing variety?***

What you are talking about is memory. What you have as an impression, content impression on your mind is coming through your physical senses. That impression is what is mostly causing the thoughts. It is causing a cohesive, consistent way that makes up for the memory. So, the variety that you observe is predominantly being registered by your mind.

When you go with your thoughts outwards, they can be as close as on the perimeter of you. You do not have to observe physically, nor do you have to be in interaction with anything or anyone else. You can be on your own, while still being stimulated by some of your thoughts. You are always having that experience within your physicality, unless you are looking within. Therefore, that variety that you are observing and creating is either outside of you, while you are actively observing with your senses, or on the perimeter of you, while you are active in your thoughts only.

That dance from within to the perimeter of you, is what the sense of variety feels like, until you take it further, from within to without, and include more in your observation with your senses also by deliberateness and purpose.

Why are there so many teachers teaching to think good thoughts? What are the thoughts?

Your thoughts are *a tool.* As well as your body, your mind and your emotions. They are telling you where you are within your creation process, and from where you are currently experiencing the creation.

There are many thoughts coming through to you at all times, and information is being exchanged at a very high speed in a form of content impression on your mind. At the same time, your body is taking trillion more sensations and impressions, and does not really get overwhelmed as much as your mind can be, based on the same process.

And so, the thought is a tool, and not really the goal for you to have. It is there for you to observe it, experience it, and choose the next one based on knowing that you are not one of your thoughts any more than the other, any more than you are any of your emotions, or your mind, or your body. That all these physical aspects are your faculties, your avenues for expression. Keeping identity with your thought, emotion, mind and body for more than fulfilling survival and basic needs exaggerates them, and therefore can cause you to feel like you have no control over them or that you are not in charge of your own creation process.

It is not that thought, emotion, mind and body are experiencing the Divine or not, it is the other way round. You are that Divine, expressing through all the available avenues and faculties, all of those wonderful tools, in order to do more of that, and to do that with as much boundlessness and bliss as is available to you. As you become aware of your blendedness from a Wider Perspective, you come to see things the way they are.

Finding a way to soften your physical faculties, including your thoughts, gets you to the point of experiencing from a Wider Perspective. From getting beyond your physical perspective for some time, and allowing yourself to choose which tool you want to express through next. Through one kind of thought or other kind of emotion, through this kind of physical activity or that kind of intellectual activity. This process of unfocusing is what brings you to lead the eternal dance you are perpetually part of anyways.

I would like to know what is the role of thoughts within the creation process. Do we attract what we think, what we give our attention to?

When you emphasize your thoughts, you get more of that and other thoughts. When you emphasize the emotion, you get more of that and other emotions. Your identification with them is what brings you more of that which you call attracting. But you are not any of those perspectives for longer than you choose to be. You are a Wider Perspective embodied and therefore experiencing those choices. Once your awareness of this is consistent, you can choose, and therefore experience what it is to *be the creation while creating as a creator.*

When you identify so much with thoughts, they represent your most predominant and active faculty, and then you feel like you need to manage them, rather than give them a rest and get to the point of a Wider Perspective for a moment.

You observe and choose, observe and choose, observe and choose—that is the segment of your creation process where your thought process contributes. Clarity of wanting is always received when you shift the gears, it always comes from a Wider Perspective. It happens when you are zooming out to a wider angle to see what is the next avenue you want to take in your experience flow. And then, it happens when you allow yourself to release even that clarity, so you can have the beautiful discovery of your wanting in your physical experience.

How do I bring the things and experiences I want faster?

Nothing brings things faster to you in your experience than the ease, and therefore, the speed in which you get the clarity of your wanting, and then release it.

Checking in more often with what you want can be that avenue for you, too. If you have such a resonance with the clarity of your wanting, that you do not go back to observe-choose mode. If you do not measure, if you do not bring the gap into your awareness, at some point you will simply be on the wave, and take the leap into discovery while riding the wave of clarity.

That does not happen as often, especially with those which you consider to be the bigger desires, something you have wanted and thought about for quite some time.

Do I even have to think about what I want?

You do not have to think at all in order to have an exuberant experience in your physicality, as your thoughts are just another way for you to express.

It is not that you need to get rid of the thoughts, but it is not necessary for you to keep repeating the same thoughts at all times in order to see your desire fulfilled. When your persistent identification with the specific thought brings the tug of war within you, it is not until you get tired and then eventually relax into less to no thoughts, that you get to experience that specific wanting show up in a physical form. It is when the thoughts are not as active, that you get the sensation and enter a fuller perspective to receive all the answers to the questions you have been asking.

You mentioned that the law of Attraction does exist. What would be your definition of the Law of Attraction?

Whatever you are observing and choosing is only the starting point in your discovery of that which is the answer, fully shaped at the moment you receive the clarity of the wanting. The answer to the question being asked is forming simultaneously, at the exact same time. And all that is happening is this beautiful dance of the inevitable cause and effect, often referred to as the Law of Attraction. Or, an even simpler way to call it is a dance between the question and the answer.

When I get the clarity of wanting, my answer is simultaneously created. How does that happen?

All that follows the moment of your clarity of wanting, is that you are ready to see something already formed within you. *That which you call creation is already within you at the time of your asking.* That feeling is already within you. That blissfulness is already within you. That awareness of a Wider Perspective is already within you. All that happens when you have the clarity of wanting, is you saying – "here it is, the clarity of wanting, and now I am going to choose an angle within me to experience it."

You might not always see it that way, but this is how it happens every single time.

Depending on how aware you are of the creation process, you may go around and do more observing and choosing, because you are looking outwards for answers. Meanwhile, all of it is within you. The clarity of the question that is coming through after the thought is involved, after the emotion is involved, after the mind is involved, after intellect is involved, after the physical body and sensation are all involved—the clarity of the question is pointing back to you to experience the answer.

Why do we always want more? Why do we always want a fuller experience?

Every particle of Everything That Exists is consistently having some kind of feedback.

Based on that feedback, there is always another angle to experience it, and by doing that, experience that which is within. As you experience more and more variety, and have all these experiences that are satisfying to you within that moment, you initiate so many of those other wants, because you want to experience that which is within from as many different angles, and in as many different ways. *This is what the full expansion is about.* It is about you experiencing everything from a different angle with the physical tools you have, in this and in every other physical iteration, and therefore bringing more of that real, blissful, satisfying discovery to you.

This all is possible because you are the process.

What do you mean by "you are the process?"

You are the process consistently pointed to a perspective of now, perspective of being, perspective of consciousness.

When you feel that you are a destination or some kind of a goal, someone you are supposed to become or be a certain way, then you are predominantly focused on those gift boxes instead of the beautiful discovery of what is in them. And because of that direction of your attention, you miss so many opportunities to discover and actually open them. There is still so much value in wrapping up more gift boxes that will wait to be discovered by you at a later time, when you are in the now. Experiencing and discovering the now, after now, after now gets you to balance the wrapping with the opening of the gift boxes. And seeing equal value in both. That balance, that equality is what makes you a process, rather than a destination.

So much of your vastness from that which you are—Divine embodied, you want to express through your physicality. And you want to always do it more, because the Divine *within you is boundless. It is infinite. It is free.* It has access to Everything That Exists, that keeps reconfiguring itself with each observation of variety by every focusing mechanism. You are looking for more of that expression, and your physicality is the tool for that boundlessness to be experienced from numerous, potentially infinite angles.

Sometimes you might experience that as some kind of question, discomfort, or dissatisfaction for a moment, but it is only to point you back more to the direction of boundlessness of you and the potential of that infinite process being experienced in the now, consistently and for all eternity.

Can we speak about a specific scenario? Kosta and I have the desire to buy a house. We know that we will, eventually, but we do not know when and how?

And so, you have been observing in all of the places you have been visiting. You have been making choices, while having various thoughts on the topic. You have been seeing possible scenarios in possible cities. That is the process of observing and choosing. You have been thinking and having emotions about it. Your mind has been dissecting and making preferences about it – "would you want to be there, would you want to be here, and for how long." That brought the clarity of that wanting, which is a house in Belgrade.

This wanting has been clear to you, and if you were not to talk about it, it would happen rather quickly. If you are to talk about it more often, depending on how much you focus on the gap there is, you go back to observing and choosing – "do you even want it, how much do you want it, and where would you want to have it?"

Every time you start asking all these additional questions, you get to the perspective of observing and choosing again, and you continue to make preferences on this topic. Your clarity of wanting the house, allowing that to be predominant so there is no more observing and choosing, is what will tip you into the direction of the discovery of your house. All the other aspects of it – how and where and when exactly – will start flooding to you. That can all be experienced within moments or longer, given your current steadiness.

The suggestion is to get to the point of experiencing the clarity of the wanting and releasing it, or to check in once in a while rather than all the time. This is how you still carve out more details of your preference, but speed up the discovery of it all together.

Do we observe variety when we sleep, too? If so, what is the difference between observing variety when we are asleep and awake?

When you sleep, you are more unfocused. However, since you are never fully unfocused for as long as you are in your physical body, your focus is still active to some degree. All of your faculties are softer, your body is softer and more relaxed, your mind is not as sharp, your emotions are way softer, and therefore your thoughts are only mildly active as well.

Depending on the state of your physical vessel, you can wake up from sleep physically depleted, fully rejuvenated or anything in between. Sleeping can be like you are meditating, or it can be like you are attempting to meditate, as some thoughts are still there.

There is too much importance given to thoughts, because they are predominant. All the brilliant teachers are trying to get you to see that there is a variety of them, available to you to choose from it. To see that there are other states of being, other emotional states you can be in, and that there are other ways for your physical body to feel because of that.

When you sleep, everything is softer. Everything. Nothing is pointed in any particular direction at the moment of your relaxation and rest. Therefore, its influence on your creation while you are in this state is so minor that you can freely put it aside.

THE QUESTION-ANSWER DANCE

The balance in Everything That Exists is based on a never-ending dance between the question and the answer.

The variety you are observing allows you to sense, and based on the feedback you gather, generate curiosities and formulate questions, or sometimes experience problems that show up in a form of various layers of discomfort. As early as you get to formulate a question and get the clarity of your wanting, you can turn your attention to the discovery of receiving an answer.

The answer is formed and available to you at the moment of getting the clarity of the question. In other words, as the question is born, the answer is born, too. As the question is formulated, the answer is revealed and out in the open. All you have to do at this point is to allow yourself to get softer in your thought and in your emotion, in an overall perception of physicality, so you can tip away your attention from a question, and notice the answer.

The clarity of wanting that you receive is the first step in your movement from the perspective of question. It directs your attention away from the perspective of a problem or any kind of negative, discomforting emotion, and moves you towards the tipping point where you start your discovery of that which is your answer.

Part 1 of the Creation Process: the movement from the question [Q] to the answer [A]. Visual 2.

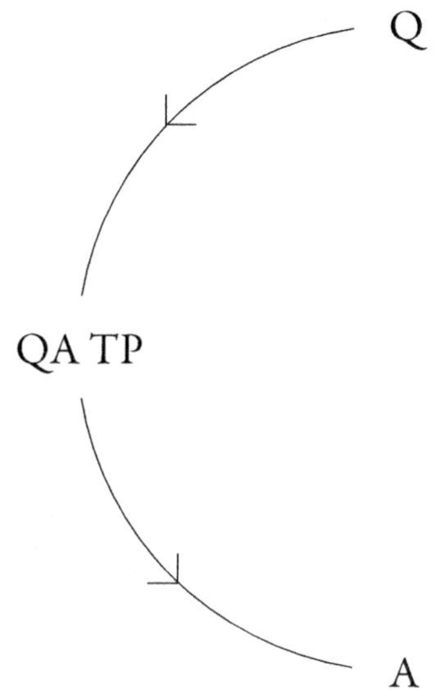

As you soften your flashlight of attention from the question [Q], you start moving towards the answer [A]. The moment of releasing the wanting is a tipping point between the question and answer [QA TP].

If you are predominantly asking questions or in a feeling of a problem, if you are mainly experiencing negative emotions, you might perceive yourself exclusively as separate from others. Yet, everything that surrounds you is *an opportunity for a reflection,* a chance to experience more through your perspective of Self. This is the step in your evolution where you expand from primarily experiencing physicality, and towards realizing your full human potential.

At various points in a day, even when you do not consciously register it, the process of releasing the focus into the softer place is happening. Prevailing moments of too much focus in one direction, given to separateness, measurement and comparison to others, are being softened up by your occasional "a-ha" moments, by your experience of clarity of wanting, by the sense of ease. Sometimes only for an instant, and then incrementally more, you get to experience the tipping point where your question turns you to discovery and discovery leads you to experience the answer. This hit or miss, feeling good or receiving the answers randomly, is the starting point for you to wonder – "How can I have more moments of satisfaction like this? How can I make this experience show up more consistently?" This is when you commence engaging in the *process of unfocusing.*

As you explore it, you start noticing that you can hold the reins of moving towards the perspective of answers, by softening up your flashlight of attention as much as your physicality allows. You notice that you can be in charge of the tipping point between question and answer, and time it on your own terms. Because you are not only physical and only Self. You are expressing that which you cannot logically explain by using your intellect. You are a Wider Perspective embodying your physicality.

The movement from the question to the answer is only one side of the creation process. While you are still in a perspective of separateness from others, you are perceiving yourself as predominantly being the question asker, and expecting someone else or something outside of you to be providing the answers. Something that sees you as equal in the creation process, even though you do not recognize yourself as equal to it at this moment, as you are not yet used to being in that Wider Perspective often enough, nor to being steady in it.

PART 2 OF THE CREATION PROCESS: THE MOVEMENT FROM THE ANSWER [A] TO THE QUESTION [Q] . VISUAL 3.

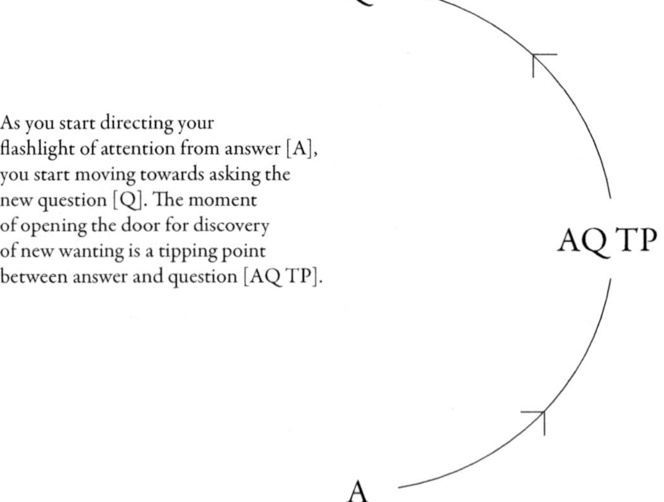

The more you get to experience positive emotions, the more you get to experience the Oneness of that which is within the abundance of an answer. When you experience love, appreciation, satisfaction, bliss, ecstasy, or thrill often enough, you start noticing that you are the life force expressing through all of your physical faculties. That is when you, and everyone else in a similar position are having the opportunity to hold the reins of the other part of the creation process.

Getting to the perspective of steadiness and ease, expressed in positive emotions you feel, is often followed by stumbling upon something else that catches your focused attention. In other words, you might feel like you are not directing the transition from being soft in your thoughts towards attention giving. You might even believe that it is not desired, nor that it is your work to voluntarily leave the state of ease and give attention outwards. While it does not have to be your effort, as your awareness of your variety will stimulate you to experience it by being curious, asking questions or experiencing discomfort or a problem – you have, at all times, the opportunity to guide that part of the process, too.

When you get to the state of ease and relaxation, when you get to the softer place of thought and you are experiencing the answer, that point is the beginning stance of the next part of your creation process. When you formulated the question, the answer was born at the same time. Now you are living the answer, and as you are experiencing it, the new question is being born, while revealing itself to be discovered by you, too. Therefore, the other part of the creation process represents you moving from the perspective of an answer, to the tipping point from which you flow into the discovery of a new question.

You can be quite deliberate, quite purposeful in guiding yourself to the answer-to-question tipping point. You do not have to find yourself in this question. You do not have to be startled by the question. You do not need to be shocked or appalled or thrown into the question. Reflections and questions do not need to leave you open-mouthed, *because you can be the one who invites them.*

So far, you might have been in this question-answer dance assuming the role of a question asker, while assuming someone else has been in the role of providing the answers. *Now you see that it is you asking questions, and you providing answers from a different perspective.* Since it is all you from different angles, you can be the one to deliberately choose how long you stay in the Wider Perspective, in your stance of being as unfocused as possible, in the position where you experience the answer.

Not holding on to it, because when you hold on, you introduce focus, you point the flashlight of your attention to variety, which results in you introducing the resistance. But you can be in that state of ease and satisfaction, listening on, acknowledging, witnessing how slowly and gradually you are moving to the perspective of giving your attention outwards. You can be the one opening the door to tip the point of an answer and consciously approach a new discovery of a new question that will give you another spin in experiencing eternally increasing bliss.

The question-answer dance is an eternal inner dance within you, at all times. You can be experiencing it from the *perspective of Self*, while seeing you are different from others. You can find more balance in witnessing that others are a *reflection of you*. And you can get to the position of such inclusivity, such a stance of a Wider Perspective applied in your physicality, that you grasp that everything that surrounds you, is not only a reflection of you, but simply a different angle of you.

THE CREATION PROCESS. VISUAL 4.

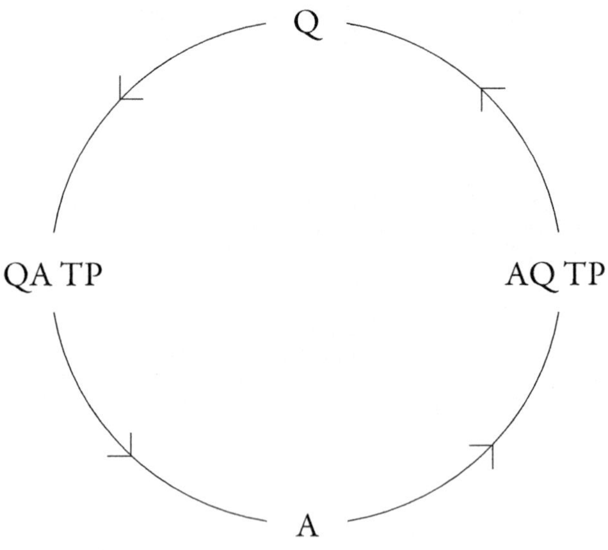

That is the time when people start saying back to you exactly what you hear within you. You experience it beyond your emotions, you encounter it beyond your thoughts. You notice it as a valuable feedback that gets you to witness eternity through physicality from more angles than Self. What you are experiencing within, but now with access to so many different lenses. That puts so much more movement and thrill, that the intensity of your enhanced and balanced physical experience brings you nothing but ecstasy and bliss along the way.

What is the question? When I am in it, what and how do I exactly ask?

The moment of formulating the question is a process not a state. Therefore, you are getting the clarity of your wanting. You are getting the clarity of what is your next discovery. What the next direction to flow your life force to and through is, so that it turns into a physical existence experienced by you.

Why do you call this question?

Because it is the process of formulating and redirecting.

All parts of the creation process described like this are tipping points. Two of them bringing the clarity – one is the clarity of a question, that moves you in the direction of the discovery of an answer, and the other one is the clarity of an answer, that moves you to formulate another question. And then the tipping points from one to another in both directions. One when you can sense that you are taking less and less focused attention on that particular topic and allowing yourself to experience its particular discovery, and when you start bringing more and more of your attention forward, therefore allowing your state of answer to densify into another question, for another turn in your eternal dance.

And how would you describe the process of answer?

As the same. The answer is revealed in the moment of your clear awareness of the question, and then you go on to discover it. In the moment of experiencing the answer, the question is revealed, and you are then on a way of discovering it. *You are in a constant and consistent state of movement.* The discovery is happening 99.99999999999% of your physical time, so the moment of clarity within the question and the moment of clarity within the answer –

while important – are so miniscule in comparison to the exuberant experience of each and every moment and each and every now that can be experienced by you in your discovery. In other words, your presence within the now brings the balance between the question and the answer so much so, that eventually you even stop making a distinction between what is what in your creation process, and you just simply are.

Do we create everything in the question? Or we create both in the question and in the answer?

In the question you are creating an answer, and in the answer you are creating the question. Therefore, you are constantly creating.

What do you mean by tipping points? Can you explain this a little bit more?

Tipping point is a position where you have been observing variety so much, that you got the clarity of the wanting. Your wanting is now so clear, that you do not feel the need to engage in an intellectual process, nor do you feel the need to give your body direction to continue sensing, and therefore to go back to the observe-choose part of the creation. You have such clarity, that you release it and start perceiving where discovery is taking you. The moment you release the wanting is when you are on the way to receive the physical version of an already revealed answer. That moment is one of the two tipping points.

On the other hand, as you are in the position of ease, love and satisfaction, you are predominantly unfocused from the variety, and you are experiencing an answer stance. At some point, while in this perspective, it is time for you to give your attention outwards. *It is time for you to go and look for some trouble. It is time for you to give rise to wanting, while not being aware of what you want just yet.* Your wanting, even though it is not yet clear what its object is, is activated when you go from the perspective of an answer and tip that point towards the place of a new question.

In other words, you release the wanting in the tipping point from question to answer, and then you activate the new wanting in the tipping point from answer to question. The clarity of wanting happens in the moment of realizing the question, but the tipping point between the answer and the new question is where your desire to want emerges.

When you say you are looking for trouble, what do you mean?

When you try to stay away from trouble, which is mostly when you are in a perspective of Self, you are comparing yourself to others and you are looking to get out of any trouble others can cause you. Over time, you develop tools and mechanisms to unfocus, and you commence to experience, and then perceive more frequently from the perspective of One. In other words, what others do you see as a reflection of you, valuable for your eternal process of understanding. Eventually, you see yourself as no separate from others, and you perceive them as you from a different angle. Then, there is no doubt it is only you who is the troublemaker, opening the door for questions to flood in.

You are not the one being startled by the questions anymore, as you are aware that you are the one inviting curiosity, wonder and question formulation. Even when your curiosity intensifies your focus so much that it brings you some discomfort, or even turns into a problem, you know how to swiftly soften it up back to a perspective of slighter discomfort, question and curiosity that leads you to an easy clarity of the wanting and its releasing into discovery.

Why would I ever want to invite discomfort?

You never want to invite the discomfort, and it is not necessary to do so, but sometimes you do by your extended focus time. Even when you are the one directing your attention outwards on purpose, tipping the point and opening the door for the new question to be hatched – sometimes, there are certain reflections coming back to you, that you might not have expected at the time.

But you always find a way. You never become a troublemaker only for a limited period of time. It is that you get to the stance of such steadiness of knowing who you are, that "uninvited" reflections do not startle you anymore. The experience of startling itself does not startle you, surprise does not surprise you, because now you know it was, it is and will always be – you. When you know you always have the tools at your disposal to get back to steadiness, you understand that variety is the only way for you to experience discovery. You become a very well versed, fully engaged professional troublemaker.

So, you celebrate variety, you go for variety, you are looking for variety, you are poking into variety, so you can experience more of that wonderful process of unveiling. Poking into variety when you feel steady means you are ready to keep yourself in a more consistent state of presence by being conscious in the now.

So, can I be in the question process and feel good and if so, how?

You can be experiencing wonderfulness at all times.

When you get to feel so steady, knowing that you can always get back to steady, you are not afraid of anything, you are not afraid to ask the questions and shake things up. You are not afraid if you are going to get into temporary discomfort, because you know you have the tools to get back to steady. Once you know you have the tools to get to steady, then you are the one opening the door for the tipping point to happen, so you go and ask the question and then you usually stay in the state of excitement and curiosity and wonder that formulates the question, and you skip the whole discomfort part.

That is what it is to be a full-fledged human.

What do you mean by steady? What does steadiness mean?
How would you describe it?

Steadiness means you know who is who in the creation process, and what perspective of you does what in the creation process. Once you know what the roles are, once you see that there is an equal value in all of them, that knowledge is what brings you steadiness.

Before you mentioned that those who are steady and inclusive see others as equal even if others do not see them that way. How is that possible, if everything is a reflection?

Not everyone is at the same stage in their evolution. Some are perceiving themselves as Self and see others as Self, too. Others move to perceive that there is Self, and that others are a reflection of them. And then there are the ones for whom the border of any separation dissipates, and they perceive that everyone and everything is them from a different angle.

This is variety at its peak. Different layers of inclusiveness coexisting as One.

Oftentimes, there is a conversation that motivation is more negative, and inspiration is more positive, so you better always be inspired. What is their role and the difference between them and where is their place in the creation process?

Both of them are a construct of your identification with your physical faculties. Therefore, whichever one works for you at the moment, you can use it in the process of formulating your question. There is no motivation and inspiration in the point of steady, there is no motivation or inspiration in the stance of feeling ease, in the perspective of receiving and experiencing the answer. Because at that moment you are simply being, you just *are.*

When you say you just are, can you expand on that state? Because sometimes, I get the sense that you do not really create when you just are. It seems kind of boring?

When you get to experience being simply conscious, being present in the moment, there is nothing to which you can compare that state of bliss. The whole creation of Everything that Exists is at the palm of your hand, as from the place of such stillness you can sense not partial, but *all* of the eternal movement at once.

Just being means simply being present?

It means being present and applying your presence into everything you give your attention to. It means experiencing wonderfulness in such a way that you are not even really making much distinction, what has been motivating and what has been inspiring you. Since motivation is the starting point, you are in the place of comparison. And inspiration is more about you following in the place of action coming out of ease. But both of them are a construct and part of your physicality.

You are constantly flowing through. You are consistently expressing a Wider Perspective. You are a life-force embodied.

THE 75/25 FORMULA

When you think about the question-answer dance that includes two tipping points, you notice the four segments within the creation process.

THE FOUR SEGMENTS OF CREATION. VISUAL 5.

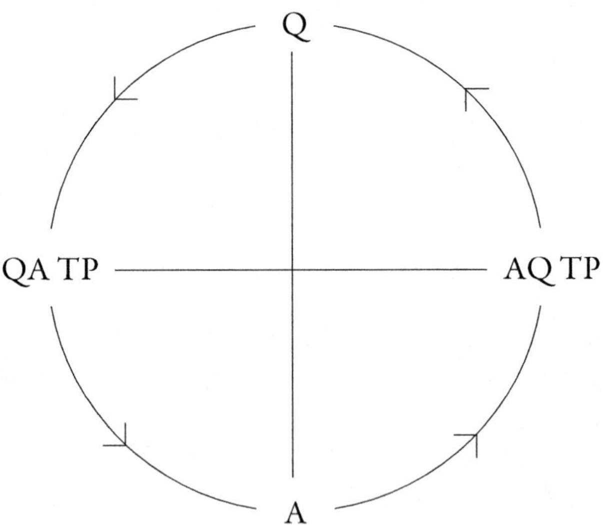

Within them, there is the potential for the majority to give you a predominantly satisfying experience. Specifically, the three of them – question to tipping point, tipping point to answer, and answer to tipping point. You can get so good at your awareness of your creation process, that seventy-five percent of your experience feels easy to you.

The 75/25 Formula. Visual 6.

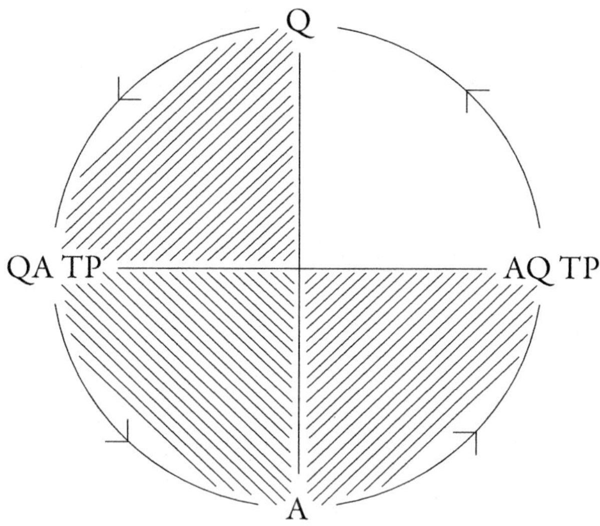

Once you get so steady and clear about the creation process, the only thing that can sometimes throw you off is the intensity of the part when you direct your focus to observing the variety, and formulating questions until you get the clarity of your wanting.

Formulating the question. Visual 7.

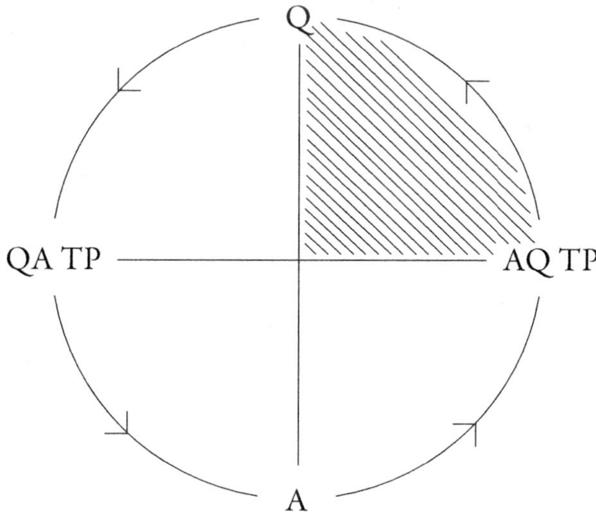

Even the ones that are predominantly in the perspective of Self, asking questions, are also experiencing a certain amount of satisfaction in their creation. They might not feel that movement from the question to the tipping point is satisfying, because they might feel like they are laboring it. Those are the ones giving too much attention to the clarity of wanting, and coming back numerous times to observe and choose on the same topic, until they witness an answer in physicality. Therefore, this segment of creation is not experienced as joyful by them.

But the moment that tipping point happens, the discovery towards the answer is always satisfying. *Always, at all times, satisfying for everyone.*

Discovering the answer. Visual 8.

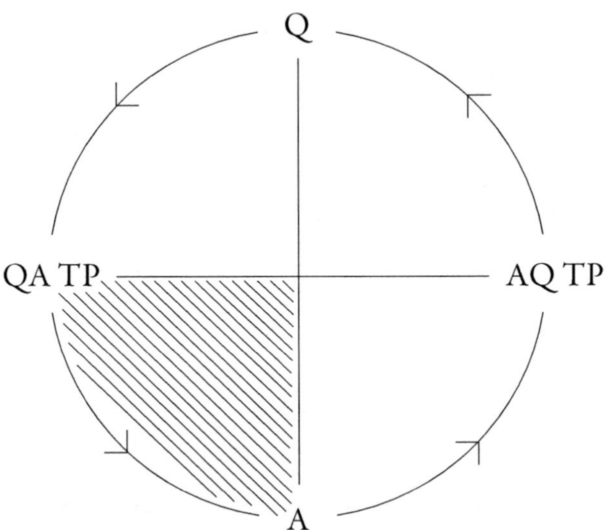

The movement from the answer towards the new tipping point can be equally satisfying as the segment before. It can be giving you more of that awareness, often referred to as milking or stretching or extending the time of satisfaction. What that means is that you do not rush into the question immediately, but rather hover a bit longer in the state of unfocus.

Applying your steadiness. Visual 9.

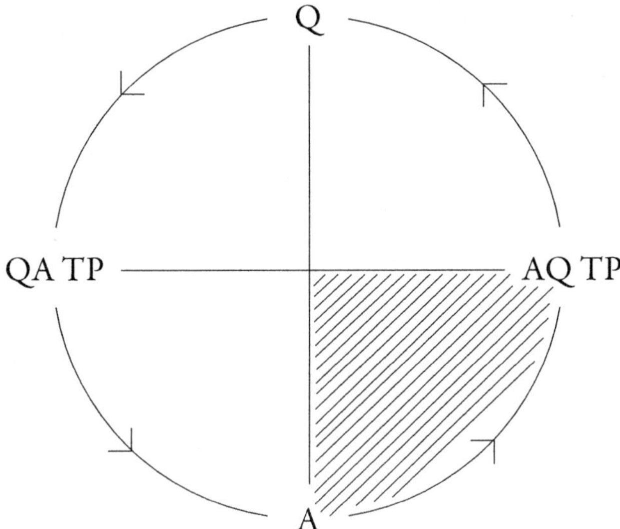

Everyone experiences questions and everyone experiences answers at all times. It is only about where you point the flashlight of your attention, and therefore experience it as your reality. Based on your awareness and your inclusiveness of you noticing yourself as separate from others, grasping others as a reflection of you, or seeing yourself as an inclusive Everything That Exists perspective embodied – you embrace the intensity of value for all aspects of the creation process.

The 75/25 formula is based upon where you are predominantly. Based on how much and how consistently you can include, and based on how often you are in the perspective of steady, ease and answer – you can grasp where you are in your own evolution.

You can enhance your steadiness to be so consistent that everything you give your attention to is wonderful. It is when you do not make a big deal out of your likes and dislikes any more. You just take the life experience that flows to you, moment by moment, seeing equal value in both.

And therefore, everything you experience is beyond your mind, body, thoughts and emotions.

What is reality?

Your choices, layers of awareness that are active, and their application to everything that you observe.

Reality is based on the perception of your inclusiveness. How separate you feel, or exclusive, or how together you feel or inclusive, or any measure of it in between. Therefore, your reality is never like anybody else's reality. And your reality now is never your reality from a moment ago or your reality in the next moment.

Everything is consistently in the movement. The way to describe reality in a short, concise way is that *reality is your own, current perspective of movement.*

What is inclusivity? And what are the benefits of it within the experience of life? Can you share an example?

As you see yourself as separate Self and you feel some positive emotion, you are experiencing it only from one angle of you, because you feel like everything and everyone else is separate. You can be having a good time, but not many around you have to experience the same in order for you to feel complete.

Now imagine that everything and everyone around you has a good time, and reflects it back to you. Then you are even more, exponentially more satisfied, as you have so much more evidence because of that reflection.

Now go even further and imagine everything and everyone else around you are you from a variety of angles. You want all of those aspects of you to be satisfied as well, so you can experience more joy, while it is simultaneously intensified by all of the angles of you.

This is what inclusivity is and what brings you to fully be human.

Why is the formula 75/25? Is it just for reference?

There is no person that does not feel relief, satisfaction, and positive emotion when they eventually release the clarity of their wanting and allow themselves to experience the answer.

During that segment of the creation process, everyone is having the experience of ease and love, of resonance and Oneness.

Similarly, everyone experiences curiosity that turns into some kind of question with more or less discomfort along the way. This is the experience from the tipping point towards the question. And therefore, everyone experiences some layer of negative emotions in that aspect of creation.

Everything else in between becomes what you make of it.

Your positive emotions are naturally easy to experience between the tipping points, on the answer side. They might start softer as a result of releasing the resistance that comes with holding attention to the clarity of wanting. Then they get fuller on the way of experiencing the answer, in which they culminate for a moment.

When you are aware you are on the way back to curiosity, in the direction towards the next tipping point, you can continue to experience all the positive emotions as they start turning into a denser, more directed focus. In other words, you can experience all of your emotions twice within each turn of your creation. Once getting towards the answer, and second time moving from the answer towards the tipping point. You can go from less to more satisfaction, and then back towards more attention, while still experiencing satisfaction.

When you go more towards the focus, it can cause you to turn curiosity into the question, and even some kind of discomfort. From the place of question, you can feel that less and less discomfort feels satisfying to you. Therefore, you can feel that by itself is a release, which you can allow more of to reach the tipping point into discovery of the answer. And then, satisfaction of receiving an answer inspires you to unveil another question, for another ride of having a predominantly positive experience.

Eventually, you get so good at this, that you stop counting at all. And then everything is bliss to you. That is when you are really experiencing your human potential in its fullest form.

CHAPTER THREE

THE POWER OF FOCUS

THE SENSE OF SURVIVAL

Every answer that every focusing mechanism has ever got, is getting, and will ever get, is being received during the process of unfocusing. For some, softening of their physical senses tends to be a rather tricky process, since an intense attention to the variety around them activates too much of that which is survival instinct within them.

This happens not only through the lens of the body looking for nutrition and safety, but also through the flashlight of their mind. For the body to be taken care of, the mind is analyzing, looking for solutions, dissecting, always wanting to organize security. And while your body cannot be without it, the mind sometimes takes over the primary role and is processing way too much information way too quickly.

To move from the perspective of seeing yourself and others as Self only is to move from activating the part of your mind predominantly focused on survival too often.

Many are not aware this is the case, as they are so in focus with their physicality, that they believe separateness is all there is. During the discovery of finding the balance from giving so much attention outwards to the feeling of consistent steadiness and conscious experience of ease, they start discovering Oneness, an Everything That Exists perspective that they are.

In your evolution from that which is simply survival, towards the awareness that there are other perspectives to explore so you can experience your full human potential, you start seeing the other, Wider Perspective of you. You first acknowledge it as someone or something else providing the answers to your questions. With time, you witness some and eventually enough evidence that unequivocally supports the knowing of who you are – an eternal awareness that has access to all the answers, at all times, within.

Why are we often in survival mode, when most of humanity has their basic needs covered?

The reason is that your mind has developed to such an extent that it has the ability of abstract thinking, it can imagine.

Throughout your evolution, you used to be predominantly a survival focused being. You can see the evidence of this evolution when observing different animals that surround you. The moment their survival needs are satisfied, meaning their food and shelter are taken care of, you witness them being easygoing, happy, and relaxed.

The process of abstract thinking also includes creating fear as the product of your powerful intellect. Your mind is exploring a variety of options, solving bigger problems, finding a variety of solutions, and getting you to think ahead. Sometimes too often. With the overuse of the mind comes the exaggeration of survival mode, and that, for many, becomes such a common experience in their creation, they start calling it natural.

Giving attention so much outwards keeps you predominantly in a perspective of Self, which, backed up by a powerful abstract thinking mind, can give you all the reasons why it is necessary to continue pitting yourself against others. Living like that, in time, you get to the point where the repetitive dance between question and question is not taking you even close to the feeling of steadiness. You may even come to experience a breaking point that brings you that awareness, but the clarity is the same. The only feasible choice is to release all the suffering, even if it is at once.

However, you do not have to be suffering at all in order to find ease. You can get there in a steadier way, with a simple awareness that your survival needs are so basic and so little, that there is no need to give it so much attention and bring other aspects of your life into the same sensation.

To experience this, you do not give survival aspects or situations attention longer than it is necessary to feel the safety and nourishment. Everything beyond that becomes a discovery, a bonus experience waiting to be explored. Everything becomes so much more joyful and satisfying because it is not driven by the experience of having to do it. Because your feeling of having to do something is always based on your over activated and overstimulated survival instinct.

There is very little that you really physically need. Everything beyond that is the clarity of your wanting that you desire to experience. When you look at the clarity of your wants, there are many more of them throughout your day than the needs necessary to be taken care of for survival. Once you see your desires as a blessing, then you have an opportunity to really explore them, rather than putting the same survival etiquette to them from a perspective of need.

Oftentimes, you feel like you have reached some point and someone else has not reached it yet, so you are looking to justify it. You put yourself in the process of justifying your experiences of goodness, by putting your desires in the same category as survival. Therefore, you bring yourself into that loop of needing so many things and experiences, instead of experiencing the joyful creation of them.

This comes from so much processing that your powerful mind is capable of, and therefore every time you get in the process of unfocusing and softening your mind, you are getting to experience from a Wider Perspective.

First occasionally, and with a little bit of practice, predominantly.

Why are there still people who lack basic resources to cover their survival needs?

When you are in a perspective of Self predominantly, you are comparing most of the time. That comparison, that exaggerated measuring is what keeps activating your survival instinct. As so many still see themselves as separate from another, they might feel that in order for that comparison to stay, they must either strive to be more than someone else, or strive to continuously compare.

Then you start looking for and justifying so many different things to do, such as wanting to pile up more, to make sure you have more so somebody else does not take it from you.

Because if you do not do something to someone else, someone else might or will do that to you. In other words, you are having the survival mode multiplied within you for no good reason.

It is all based on fear, and all of the fear is the construct of your mind, of you not having balance within your own focus and unfocus dance.

And so, they are the ones feeling like they need to do this for someone else. And then they are the ones who feel someone else needs to do that for them. The balance is really about everyone starting to see that they are more than just separate entities. More than someone in the lack and someone in the surplus, someone who needs assistance, and someone who is looking to provide that assistance to others.

Everything that everyone is doing, even if it feels like it is mean or evil, or forced upon you, is because they believe that they are helping. They genuinely believe that what they are doing is really beneficial to you, because you cannot do it for yourself.

But when you get to see that it is not you trying to tell something to someone else, but it is you trying to tell that to yourself, and you experiencing that as a reflection back to you, once you start pulling often enough to a Wider Perspective by any process of unfocusing that gets you there, once you check in with that perspective more often, you then start seeing that everyone and everything around you, is you.

Then you start cheering for everyone else around you. That is when you start improving and evolving everything around you, because you know that is all you as well. Because you know that it is not only you and then someone else, that it is not even you and a reflection of you that helps you get where you want to get. *But that it is all you from a different angle.*

Once you understand that everything is you, then you can clearly experience that which is Oneness, that which is in the essence of Everything That Exists.

What is fear, and why does fear exist?

Certain, small amount of fear is necessary for your survival. Your complex system between the body, the mind and your emotions is consistently giving you feedback on what you need in order to keep yourself in balance. And while some of that discomfort is necessary for you to keep paying attention and looking for new layers of balance, that which is extreme fear, shown through extreme negative emotions (representing different layers of fear), is the consequence of you giving so much attention outwards, and therefore replicating more of survival instinct experience than you really need to.

The fear is really you worrying about something in the future, that may or may not happen.

That comes to be your experience when you are too reactive, when you are looking to get ahead of so many things. In attempting that, you focus too much on the destination, and not necessarily on the process of getting there. And when your focus is so much on the destination, it delays your arrival to it almost every time, while exaggerating your attention back to survival mode.

On the other hand, you can get to those destinations you desire by having full harmony with Everything That Exists embodied in your physical environment, including everything and everyone along the way. You can have tremendously blissful experiences, or you can be in a survival instinct for too long. Until you cannot handle it anymore, and until you give up the struggle because you finally release the focus, and therefore receive the answers.

Sometimes, you might feel that because you are suffering through, eventually you receive your desires, which is never the case. It only appears to be that way, because after so much intense focus you eventually, and rather quickly, have to unfocus from suffering as you cannot handle the exaggeration of your outwardly focused perspective anymore.

If you pay close attention, you can see that there are many who always create through suffering, and predominantly through the place of survival instinct, but also the ones who have a blissful time while creating, due to their own resonance and clarity of their perspective of steady.

Can the survival mode totally disappear? No!

You have answered your own question. There will always be something to provide you with the feedback. The moment that there is no necessity for your survival, you fully unfocus and you are ready for the next fresh perspective in the form of a new physical iteration.

Why do people decide to be fully focused in a variety of ways?

There are some who have been trying to push focus to such limits that it is truly overwhelming for them. They build up so much of that focus outward, and in that involve so much of intellectual processing, that the structure of their physical vessel cannot support it anymore.

And then there are the ones who do it in a softer way, the ones who gradually and consciously get to know that variety has served them sufficiently, and then they are ready for a fresh perspective. The ones who might even start getting bored with the variety that surrounds them, because they are so steady within their experience that they start looking for trouble. Until even that is not exciting anymore, and it brings a desire for a fresh clean slate of experiences. In other words, they are ready to start the whole satisfying game all over again.

What would you call death? And how does this transition happen?

Closing one door and opening another. It is just a continuation of the movement from current to a different vantage point.

THE INTELLECT

You have been evolving to such a degree that more of you have been finding yourselves not so physically involved, not so physically spent throughout the day, and still comfortably providing for all the basic necessities for your physical experience.

This is because, instead of your body, you have been using more of your mind, particularly your intellect to bring more efficiency, and therefore ease in your expression of life. In a way, you have conquered your body by using more of your mind to bring forward your creation.

One's focus on the body predominantly brings the experience to be about Self only, mostly comparing, and therefore in a survival mode. Your movement from seeing yourself as an individual only, to seeing others as a reflection of you is in direct correlation with your body dominance shifting to mind leading the way. By using the frame of your mind more, you start seeing the glimpses of others being a reflection of you.

And so, as humanity gets to move within the range of what is known into what is unknown, you have the opportunity to practice that which is the process of unfocusing. The evolution that you are experiencing, even right now, the movement that you are sensing with so many being able to be focused around similar or same topics instantaneously, regardless of where they are in the world, your interconnectedness with others – it is all showing you how everything is always a reflection of you.

The speed of your evolution got you to move and shake up your beliefs that there is only Self and another Self. Your intellect, its usage, exploration and the awareness of your mind got you to experience that others are your reflections. It brought you to the doorway of witnessing how Everything That Exists is being applied to your physicality. To experience full inclusiveness from a Wider Perspective, you are to use the tool of your *emotions*.

By being aware of them, and using them as a guidance, a pointer to where you are in your creation process, you can allow yourself to enter a Wider Perspective sufficiently enough. There, you do not see and identify yourself with your body or mind, and therefore with those emotions either. This is when your whole physical construct is being witnessed as a tool, rather than the main aspect of you, and you experience yourself as One with everything and everyone around you.

> ***What is a mirror reflection? How does it apply to our lives? For example, a tree is an object of my attention, and therefore a reflection. Do I create that tree? How does mutuality work and how can we see the benefits and value of it? How can we move from the mutuality that we do not want to experience and enter a new one?***

You are starting with the premise of liking and disliking.

Yet, everything is a reflection of you, regardless of whether you like it or not. And there is an equal value in liking and not liking. Even though it might seem like it, you are not looking to eradicate not liking and have only liking experiences. When you are aware of who you are, of what your faculties and tools that express you as a life are, you stay in each of those likes and dislikes for as long as you need to and choose to.

It is not about eliminating and eradicating. It is about reflection and feedback of more coming to you. Whatever you have going on within you as a process is consistently reflecting back to you. When you are so focused in your body, in your mind, thoughts and emotions, you do not necessarily see that. You see someone else. You see yourself different from other people, nature and things, and you do not really even see that there is much value, because your attention is predominantly on your own physical faculties.

When you start being perceptive, you sense everything and everyone else. That means you are not only giving attention to your process of physicality, seclusion and exclusivity, but are also really soaking in *all of your reflections* through your senses.

When you go and observe the tree, or you go and observe an animal without any particular reason why, without looking for any kind of outcome, your perception of it can tell you the reflection that is coming back to you. It is the same with observing people. They are the ones you are comparing yourself to, by measuring, having them as a starting point of motivation for you to receive answers that fuel your inspired action. While you are giving your attention to everything and everyone, they can provide you with all of that valuable feedback when you are open to perceive.

These reflections are always, at all times, available to you. On the other hand, they can be of benefit to you once you are sufficiently aware that you are not only Self, that you are not only physical. Once you start seeing that you have so many identities and roles you play, and that they are shifting throughout the day, every day. A variety of roles based on what you are experiencing at that moment in your body, in your mind, thoughts and emotions.

Once you stop holding on to that which is a secluded aspect of Self, you start seeing what others are reflecting back to you. Sometimes you might not like it, sometimes you might really enjoy it. Once you see that there is an immense value to them, *you cannot unknow what you know.* You cannot go back to pretending that you are separate from others. Then, it becomes only about finding consistency and choosing the speed in seeing the value. To be able to be so steady, that you are always on a lookout for the value that is coming based on that reflection.

Even when you do not see the value immediately.

Sometimes, when you get a positive reflection, you open up its value rather quickly. On the other hand, when you have a negative reflection, you do not see the value at that time. *Knowing that there is value even when you do not see it will allow you to shift back into the process of unfocusing, and get yourself to the perspective from which you are able to see that value.*

You always see, in detail, all of the steps of your creation in retrospect. Once you recognize that you have experienced what once was a desire, if you are curious to see how you got there, you can see all of the steps that brought you to that experience. But never really all of the steps ahead. Because when you try to do that, you involve your physicality, you involve your mind that wants to dissect and project and organize and solve. Therefore, your ride becomes a little bumpier, wobbly, and your desire shows up to your experience with delay or not at all.

Oftentimes, I hear the word unconditional – "be unconditional, love unconditionally," but then even within that context, I was hearing it as "unconditional equals feel good." Then I thought that even feeling good is also a condition. Then you mentioned doing it for no reason. What is unconditional versus conditional and how does that apply to the creation process?

You are always having some kind of tools or conditions to carry your physical experience, so it is safe to say you cannot be physical without the conditions.

To get to the perspective of that which you call unconditional or all-inclusive in the experience, is to be able to see everything and everyone represents you from a different angle, while pointing more of you back to you. In other words, you now have eyes not only through your own lens of physical experience, but through all of these other people, animals, nature and objects that you are mutually interacting with. You are providing all that consistent feedback back to you.

When you are predominantly in a place of question, you do not want any of that feedback, you want tools and conditions to get you to steady. And while that in itself can be very satisfying to you, it is still a hit or miss experience, based on what potential you are unlocking to experience from the perspective of steady. Based on how much application of that steady, that Everything That Exists in your experience is happening and therefore showing itself in your environment as the physical evidence.

When you get to the perspective that your conditions and tools are consistently getting you to steady, then you can test out your steady in an unconditional way.

To get to steady, when you are not, you will always use a condition. But the other side of the creation process is where you can experience unconditionality by not being startled by the question, but by you being the one that opens the door for it. That part of the creation process is the unconditional part, where no matter what you give your attention to, everything feels wonderful because you know that there is value for each and every aspect of your creation. *This is what it means to be unconditional.*

It is when you are not looking for any condition to keep you steady. Because you cannot keep steady or experience love, or any positive emotion while holding on and while having a condition. You use the condition to get you to steady but *then you release* the condition for you to experience the fullness of Everything That Exists flowing through you in all of its expressions.

There is nothing more unconditional than you being steady and then deliberate, purposefully opening the door for new questions to lead you to a little bit of self-invited trouble.

LIVING BEYOND EMOTIONS

How would you describe emotions? Where do they come from, what is their role within the creation process, and how do you currently see this evolution of balancing body, mind, and emotions?

Your feelings or emotions are the tool for you to know in which part of the creation process you are. A very valuable tool that you have at your disposal. However, still the tool, as they do not make for who you are, nor do they make up for your identity.

When you feel predominantly negative emotions, you exaggerate the question at hand, and therefore discomfort or fear of certain kind shows up. Then you want to move on to the other side of the creation process, so you can experience more of those, for now rare moments of feeling good or steady. So you start seeing more value in positive emotions then negative, because you have not experienced them as much.

This is an inevitable part of your evolution, for as you were moving from the perspective of predominant focus in your body and mind, your emotions have been settling in as a tool for your expression, so you find more of that resonance and balance beyond just the simple survival.

Your feeling system always tells you what you have going on at that moment, but trying to own or to identify yourself with just one kind of emotion, regardless of how good or not good it feels, is still *the process of holding on.* Which means experiencing more of your focus outwards and keeping your intellect and your mind so active that it sometimes shows up in your body in a form of some kind of discomfort or pain.

For you to find more balance is to understand that your body is a tool which you have been evolving, your mind is a tool that you have been developing like never before and now, the next logical step is to find that balance within the emotions, knowing that there is so little necessary for your survival. That there is so little need to activate those extreme emotions on both sides of the spectrum, and that you can find more balance that is projected by you. Once you start seeing the emotions as an inevitable tool, you tend to choose what is more natural for you through your physicality, and that is observing the variety that gives you some kind of question, or discomfort, or dissatisfaction, and then moving towards predominantly having that which is a blissful state of being.

The only way to get there is to see yourself, your physical structure including your emotions, from a little bit of a distance. By using the process of unfocusing, to witness that you are not the mind, nor the body nor the emotions, but a life force that uses those physical faculties as your tools for expression. The moment you are there, you make beautiful relationships with your emotions, mind, and body. You start using them in the most efficient, balanced and satisfying way, and your life experience becomes so satisfyingly intensified, that you are blissful all around, moment after moment, after moment.

Your physical design has the potential and all the necessary tools for a full-fledged human experience.

It is a vessel that can take you way beyond the dimension of Self. Everything that you are composed of, all of the particles within you, are predominantly filled with the Wider Perspective or what is often referred to as the non-physical, Divine dimension. Since that potential is within every cell of your body and physicality around you, it is only with the practice of unfocusing that you can get to the place of experiencing that dimension, too.

Then you experience this Divineness of you as your predominant aspect, and you can really experience the whole Cosmos, Everything That Exists within you, because it exists within every single part of you. Within every single particle that is a part of you, or part of others, that are also part of you. You start seeing no limits even in your physical experience. You witness Oneness with so much clarity that everything, including your emotions, keeps assisting you to experience more of it.

So many brilliant teachers make you aware of your emotions being the tool, but not the destination. In the beginning, it is good for them to be your destination, for you to experience more of that which you have not experienced before. Then you can move on from a temporary destination that was there only to show you possibilities, to a perspective that you can have in every moment, as you are balancing your own question-answer, focus-unfocus, positive-negative emotion dance.

What do you mean by living beyond emotions and how is that process applied to our existence?

Your existence is so vast, and at the same time so within you. It really goes beyond your physicality. Once you experience the resonance with the life force you truly are, you go about it, not without the emotions, but *beyond the experience of those emotions identifying and defining you.* You go beyond the experience of your thoughts being you. Beyond the experience of your mind and body being you. *You see them all as avenues for expression.*

Living beyond emotions is getting to the wider place where you are not waiting for different thoughts to drop to you, not waiting for different emotions to drop to you, nor for those desires to come and drop to you, but you are the one that includes them into your presence.

By experiencing more of a Wider Perspective, your zoomed-out perspective, you include more and more and more of that vastness. In other words, you are looking within and getting to a Wider Perspective and then choosing which pipeline of thought, emotion, intellectual process or physical activity you want to activate next.

To live beyond the emotions, to live beyond the mind and body and apply it to physicality is to experience this Wider Perspective several times throughout each day. With the process of finding your physical senses, emotions and intellect to be softer, your perception comes through. So, in everything you give your attention to, you also perceive Oneness.

When we perceive Oneness through all our physical senses, how would you describe that state we are just in? And do we experience the ultimate satisfaction in that state?

In that experience of you simply being, or just being present, you are experiencing a state of bliss that cannot be compared to any emotion that you try to identify with, no matter how good it feels.

You transcend the feeling of physicality into a totally new perspective.

When you are feeling so much resonance with the ease of your own steadiness, all of your physical cells are bursting with bliss, because of the balance that they are experiencing. Such balance between the question and the answer, that it does not even feel like a ride. It feels like a perspective of such balance that stillness is the only way to describe it.

Blissful in the moment, physically focused from a Wider Perspective, experiencing that which is your full human potential.

CHAPTER FOUR

YOU INSIDE AND OUT

Your physical vessel is an accumulation of everything that happened before you. Your body is an accumulation of all of that which came even before you focused into this physical reality, into that which you are experiencing now. All that your ancestors were bringing through their thought process, awareness and imprints that showed in their sensory systems. Therefore, not only that you have picked up their stories, their ways of living, their thought patterns, the context in which you have been brought up, but you carry information about the whole evolution through your own very physical aspect of the body.

And so it is safe to say that you are, at this moment, at the peak of everything that has ever existed, having the access to everything that has been with the full potential of what is ahead. And so, your resemblance to your ancestors is not only in the physical aspect, but you are also a temporary conclusion of everything that has been evolving. Temporary, because there are no conclusions, and you are constantly evolving. And so, your body vessel is absorbing everything that surrounds you, even within this and every other physical iteration, way more than your flashlight of attention can bring in to your mind consciously.

To be in the perspective of now, to be in the stance of simply being, that full-fledged human experience is an attainable experience for anyone. It is your birthright. The variety that leads to it is based on all of these eternal contexts embodied in you. And so, at all times, you have a choice of being either what was before, as you are bringing more of it into your physical experience, or to have the experience of your design in deliberately selecting approaches to nurture your body.

Your physical cells are self-regulating at all times. They are continuously changing. They are having their own question-answer dance, looking for more and more balance, until at some point they re-emerge so they can experience physicality from a new vantage point.

The consistency you are experiencing is because of your choices. Everything within you is consistently looking for that which is balanced and directed through your flashlight of attention. Attention and not thought, as that which you direct as your attention can be experienced through your body, mind, thoughts and emotions. But it does not have to. It can be directed within and towards your inner, yet Wider Perspective.

You are the conductor of the orchestra of millions, billions, trillions, an infinite number of cells that are a part of you, coming in, through and out of you and then moving on to be part of someone or something else. Even in your physicality, while not fully clear to your eyes, *the Oneness is happening at all times.* What was part of you becomes part of someone else, what was part of someone else becomes part of you — all through your own directing skills of the tune that you want to be playing.

That which is often referred to as frequency or vibration or oscillation, is continuously bringing you the awareness that you are a complex system of simple sounds. Therefore, you can tune it up based on where you are at that moment by the attention you are giving. You are a tune. You are a tuner that you are tuning for the tune you want to experience. But you are also *a tuning process.* Therefore, everything that you are experiencing is really this wonderful balancing act that can be so satisfying throughout.

Your physical vessel is brilliantly orchestrated, so much so that the survival part is taken care of with less and less effort through your instincts. You do not need to be aware of all of the processes within your brilliant physical vessel. You are only to listen to your physical body, as its nourishment and nurturing needs very little.

Your body is a platform, it is the potentiality for you to experience various dimensions, while in the physical body. Not only to experience your existence from the perspective of Self, but to dance towards your *innate nature* that everything is a reflection of you and therefore a different angle of you at all times. When that reflection is soft, genuine and kind, or when that reflection seems a little harsh, you perceive all of it from a new angle of your own question-answer dance.

Therefore, listening to your body vessel can be interpreted as the basis for all of your spiritual experience.

Self-discovery starts with your body, with listening to what kind of fuel it is looking for, and seeing the systems you are applying to bring it to the most efficient place of least resistance and traction. Only in that kind of environment can all of the other dimensions be accessible for you to experience. To be on a spiritual journey is to consistently be aware of how your body is finding balance so your mind can get to that state of being as well.

The physicality of your vessel is brilliant, self-regulated, self-organized, and with the potential to be available to you for as long as you have interest to stay in your physical iteration. You can witness the evolution and nurturing of the body and its effect on increasing life expectancy, not only due to technology and medicine but also because of your awareness. It is because of your *awareness* that your body can be more effortless, so it can continue to represent the platform for your satisfying, integrated life experience.

> ***When we are born, is our physical appearance based on the genetics of our parents, or do we choose the physical appearance and characteristics like the nose, eyes, etc. by observing the environment?***

It is always a mutual experience. When you come through physicality, as the product of your parents' genetics, you inevitably take on certain characteristics, not only from your parents, but from all the generations before. You see that in examples where certain generations have certain physical appearance, and some skip but then some continue bringing it on. Sometimes, people are surprised by the color of the eyes in the families, since generations before no one had had it. It can trickle down through many generations, not only through the ones that you are giving attention to because they are still physically focused.

In that sense, you can trace so many characteristics coming through based on your eternal question-answer dance, and now having new physical iteration as a fresh starting point. And so throughout your life experience, you have an opportunity to look and to mold into whatever your preference becomes. Not only through technology and medicine, but also through your awareness. That which is continually coming through you for eons has a certain perspective, momentum, a certain direction, because you have been experiencing it. But you have an opportunity to have the feeling of resolve, resonance, freedom, and of the abundant feeling of satisfaction, by choosing to shift some of those generational and genetic predispositions.

Those contexts have been equally embodied into your genetics through observation and storytelling, as they have through your physical movement and manifestation into the physical matter. And so you can change all of those stories. They are a starting point, and therefore affect the balance of your chemistry in your body that is expected to operate a certain way based on all of the statistics prior to your coming into this physical iteration.

All of the habits, all of the ways of behaving, all of it is susceptible to change. You never choose those experiences from your genetics to be copy paste experiences for you, too.

> ***So how do I shift my genetics? I have heard many teachers encourage us to tell the story the way we want it to be. By doing that, I have experienced more ease and a shift in my beliefs and in my physical experience. But I am curious, from a scientific point of view, how does that happen? How does the process happen throughout the thought, changing the story, the belief, and then the energy of it changes and then that materializes?***

You are the director of your orchestra of trillions of cells that are consistently looking for an experience more balanced than that of the ancestors before you. As you take whatever condition or physical appearance, or the state of mind, or the emotional experience, you take all of that as a starting point, and starting point only.

For when you accept it as something that is your destiny, when you accept that it is something that you have to experience because someone else has experienced that before, when you accept that there is something that you do not have much control of, that you do not have any say in, then you stick mostly within that which is the context that was inherited by your physical experience. Even then, your life experiences are always shifting and molding, regardless of how much you are involved to change them. In acknowledging where you are at, you can accept it forever or choose for that to be the starting point only. From that position, you discover what you want to keep and what you would like to reshape, without the pressure of timelines, without the pressure of anything needing to happen, since you can have a balanced experience with the way cards have been given to you anyway.

Those aspects of you that you see in your ancestors and that you want to adjust, you want to take them only as a starting point. And see what of that sticks around in your new mixed context based off of where you are giving your attention. Because it is your *attention* flowing through your thoughts, emotions, and intellect of your mind vessel, as well as through your physical perception and senses, that is the one thing directing it all.

The position you might be calling *Inner Self or Inner Being* is the point of view that is directing it all, at all times. It is your Wider Perspective, wide enough to show you there is the space between you and your physical vessel. To show you that you are not any of those physical lenses, but the *light behind them.*

When you commence to consistently operate from that position, everything is moldable, everything is changeable because you are aware that you are *the One,* the Divine part of you, the light part of you captured by your choice within this specific physicality to experience it by having it at your disposal as a tool, a mechanism for your expression.

This is when you are able to change your psychological structure to your liking, to adjust and choose the time spent in each of your emotions, to adjust your intellectual processes and their efficiency, and also to change your physical body one deliberate pointing of the flashlight of attention at the time.

> ***Many refer to the Inner Being or Inner Self as a separate entity. But since we have already talked in previous chapters about that, I would love to shed some more light on the concept of the Inner Being. What is it and how does it work with body and mind?***

As your perspective outwards is more dominant, you might be predominantly thinking that is all there is. By predominantly observing and choosing from variety, you might not be releasing that which is the clarity of wanting, and your attention may stay there long enough that you do not check in with the Wider Perspective often enough to be reminded of who you are.

It is not that you are a physical body or the mind or a thought or emotion that has an Inner Self perspective. *Your Inner Self perspective is expressed through all of these physical tools.*

In your discovery of that which consists of every time you ease up, every time you are relaxed, every time you are satisfied, every time you are happy, every time the positive emotion overcomes you, every time you feel any sense of relief, every time you release the resistance, every time that you are softening up the intensity of the flashlight of your attention pointed to your physical senses of the body or the mind, active emotion or a thought that is activating the emotion, you start *shifting*, and you start calling that a different state, a fuller perspective of you. This *Wider Perspective* is not the Wider Perspective that you are not a part of, not the Wider Perspective dedicated to someone else and not to you, it is just your Wider Perspective compared to how you observe physicality.

Because this Wider Perspective is within you, it is referred to as the Inner Self or Inner Being, Divine, God, Source, Energy, Love. It is embodied in physicality, looking to express itself in everything it gives attention to, through every tool that it desires to flow through at the time.

Boundless experience, looking to stretch and expand the boundaries of physicality from a point unique only to you.

This is who you are.
And so that is why more, that is why longer life expectancy, that is why more efficient mind, that is why more satisfying emotions, that is why thoughts computed at exponentially faster speed – for all of your desires to express more quickly.

That which you might refer to as your Inner Self, is you. You reflecting you from inside out, expressing it. This has always been your thing. It is just that sometimes you get too close to the lenses, so it might appear that those lenses are what makes for all of you.

> ***Where does physical life start? When we are born, when we are in the womb? How does that all happen?***

There is a process of integrating and blending. For as you were in a physical iteration, reemerged into full unfocus and now you are ready to focus again, so it takes a moment for you to reemerge.

That which is a true connection, that which is a true, full integration, happens when that integration has mutually satisfied both the ones that are carrying the new life, and the new life ready to express itself. Sometimes that decision is clear from the moment of initial experience of integration. Sometimes it takes a moment for it to be established. So, it varies based on the ease in mutuality, on the physical experience and physical stability of the person carrying the life, too.

You can think of it as a relationship being made. Sometimes it happens immediately, at first sight, clearly to be a mutual relationship for the rest of the physical iteration. It is exactly the same process in life, coming to be in physical form with a parent.

Sometimes life is looking for expression, for integrated experience, and it is not ready. And sometimes it is so easily ready, that it is clear from the get go that the expression will be there to stay. It is one of the aspects that you try to understand through the frame of your mind, and wider dimensions of your experience give you more clarity on when you get to be there predominantly.

In most cases, it is first easier to recognize the Inner Self, your Wider Perspective, as something that is not you, as you have identified with your physical body so much that you might perceive other dimensions of life as something that is not you, something that is separate from you.

When you see yourself predominantly from the perspective of Self, you most often feel that there are not that many answers or solutions flowing through. When you have been predominantly in that perspective, and you recognize there are other positions available, you start shifting and seeing enough answers as the evidence of the potentiality of different outcomes. At that time, you might be observing God, Source, Universe as someone you have just found, someone else who is providing the answers.

In other words, you can observe it from a distance and see its value. You then see that there are not only questions to be asked, but that there are also answers coming through when you look towards this Wider Perspective.

With time, you get to witness more of the evidence of that Wider Perspective being within your reach. On your own terms. At your own pace and time. It might feel like you are merging with your Wider Perspective, but what happens is that you merge with your own body, you settle into a position you have always wanted to be in while in this and every other physical iteration.

And then you are clear about the thrill you had about your physical experience, that you have got entangled with so much by keeping your flashlight of attention outwards. Entangled in the thrill of discovery that sometimes brought you too much sensory focus.

Then you start comparing from your Wider Perspective, you experience physicality from that Wider Perspective and eventually you get to the place of undeniably knowing that you have always been operating from that wider angle, regardless of your level of awareness of it.

> ***I have been experiencing and having more awareness in observing my mind. Even when I get these moments of things not happening, I start to remind myself that this is normal, because this is my mind's function. And then that creates a certain space for me to soften up back to my awareness.***

As you get through your flashlight of attention, through your brilliant *mind*, you activate *thoughts*. When you predominantly put your flashlight of attention through your *body*, you have an *opposite experience*. When you predominantly have awareness of your body, you listen more to the activity of your body. And you usually get to unfocus more easily when the flashlight of your attention is on your body than when it is on your mind.

To get into the position of observing any aspect of your physicality as a lens for expression, you want to be in a p*rocess of unfocusing*. To be there, your body and your mind want to be softer in their activity.

When you offer too much intellectual stimulation to your mind, it is harder for you to unfocus than when you offer that same intensity of focus to your body. Activating the body while being physically alert is what makes people kind of addicted to their physical activity, as it gets them to feel balanced. In the state of physical activity, when the body is being directed to more awareness about its energy flow, the mind inevitably softens up.

Not because the mind is not active, but because the body is more active.

In the variety of beliefs on how to quiet the mind, *physical activity or activity that is bringing awareness towards your body,* regardless of how many calories are spent, is really there to get you to the place of easing up the mind. This is because of the body awareness; your flashlight of attention is pointing more towards the body and therefore the mind can ease up.

This is why the physical movement of the body that allows energy to flow deliberately precedes every successful breathwork.

Successful in terms of you using the breathwork to soften up the mind activity, so you can see a little bit more clearly and therefore take another leap. So you can pull wider and disperse your flashlight of attention and choose where you want to point it and express next.

This is what it means to be pulling into a Wider Perspective, or pulling into the full perspective of who you are, which is often referred to as the Inner Being or Inner Self.

Once this happens and is recognized, all it takes is the trust in the process of building consistency. As sometimes your mind will trick you. Sometimes even your body will trick you. You really want to listen, especially when you have experienced something different in your awareness of getting to a Wider Perspective.

And next time when your mind or body tells you that that might not be the way for you, still trust that process because that process is consistently the same. Sometimes you will dedicate the time and it will not happen. Sometimes you will dedicate the time and *it will* happen. But the process of what brings you more of that awareness at all times is *consistency*. The experience of your steady life force expressing through everything that you give attention to requires a little bit of practice.

This is really what *the choice* is all about – how consistently you want to have those experiences, and therefore make that your predominant way of expressing.

First you see the potential, by interacting with the ones that do the work and also offer their tools that got them to their consistency. The choice of you taking your steps is always yours.

You have an opportunity, in every physical iteration, to have that which is a full human experience. *You expressing through all of your physical senses, as a full-fledged human being.* Not you choosing between having the Wider Perspective or physical perspective, but blissing in your blended experience throughout.

Since there is one Wider Perspective, why do explanations coming from different receivers (like Kosta) sound a little bit more complex? And sometimes maybe not as general as you? Is it the intention of each person receiving? How does that all work?

The intention is the same for everyone who has been exploring different dimensions and finding a variety of angles that they can express this through.

The intention is the same, finding this possibility for themselves first, and choosing whether or not to broadcast to others. For many, the effect on them has been so transformative that they would want everyone else to benefit from it as well. How far they get depends on their steadiness.

Not everyone will benefit from that which everyone flows through in a form of an answer. But it is providing a unique opportunity from a unique angle that has not been offered before.

And so it has to do with interest. It has to do with eagerness. It has to do with steadiness. It has to do with daily practices. It has to do with prioritizing, and it has to do with how wide the attention can be pulled away to encompass and capture as much of the infinite perspective of Everything That Exists.

That is what I thought, that it is the person's choice of what is more exciting for them to share?

It is their choice, not in the sense of what is more exciting, but how wide the perspective they want to include. In other words, from how many different angles they want to see it, from how many different experiences, including their physicality, they want to witness it. It is *the thirst* that is brought by the variety observed, that brings more of this desire. Everyone is hooked up to the same library, allowing a different angle of it, not more or less of it. But a different angle and consistency that is coming through and resonates with the ones that are interacting with the receiver. Personal desire of how many angles they will provide is based on their own preference and on their own discovery.

Since stretching of the Wider Perspective is at all times eternal and limitless, if Kosta's and my intention is to continue stretching and stretching and stretching, will there be infinite angles that we are going to flow and share with others?

Your intentions have brought this work to life.

Your questions and your thirst for all of these questions to receive answers, together with Kosta's desire to be a vessel and represent a steady experience for others, so they find more of their own resonance – for everyone to win at all times – is a combination that is unique in its nature. So much so that it is very rare, and brings so much value, not only to the two of you, but to everyone who is interacting while asking or formulating questions.

Therefore, many experiences will keep bringing so much more variety to be observed and chosen, and that will translate to many questions, and therefore deepen the number of different angles from which these reflections can flow.

Why do we love to do this work? It seems that my answer to these questions comes from my intellect, and I would like to hear your answer from a Wider Perspective. Every single project we do absolutely has the same intention behind it, which is to offer people different tools to experience their own nature.

Your thirst for inclusion is what brings your work to life. Your thirst to witness more of that inclusion. You are bringing not only the tools, but *a steady perspective.*

Your steadiness in awareness of a Wider Perspective flowing through you, and Kosta, and everyone around seeing more of that Oneness.

In other words, what you are looking for is to experience in action more of that which you are. Then it is no surprise you want others to be in on that, because the bigger the party, the more fun and satisfaction along the way. The more you witness others in their steadiness, not as a reflection, but as you from a different angle – the fuller you get to be in your human beingness.

That is what being whole feels like.

Another thing I am curious about. I was having a sensation that even if we lie, we cannot lie.

When you are lying you are pretending you are not Divine.

That is your mind chopping things up. Because the body might have had some kind of sensation, or some kind of habit, habitual thought, or habitual context. But when you are aware, from your perspective of who you are, you are consistently inclusive in Everything That Exists. You do not pretend. You go about your life like everyone can hear everything you think, not only everything you say, at any time. And you are confident about it. When you get to that place of understanding of what your nature really is, that is the only time you can be all-inclusive. Therefore, that is the time when you are not covering any mirrors.

It is inevitable that you will go to a position of judgment sometimes. That is what lying is. Sometimes getting into the perspective of making an opinion. It is inevitable to sometimes be in that position, but when you are aware of who you are, you know you can predominantly be in a perspective where you just dip in for curiosity and to formulate a new question and not longer than that. In other words, you will not give it identity and air time, as you will not be holding on to any identity exclusively.

You will be dancing between them, and therefore consistently be aware of the identity of your nature, which is your brilliant life force expressing.

What else can I ask about the mind?

Your mind is a platform for you to perceive your thoughts and the emotions.

It is a tool you use to process what you are perceiving in your physical senses, and to make a choice what to give attention to.

Your mind is a very important tool for making preferences and choices. But when it is overstimulated, it gives you an illusion that your preferences and choices are all that there is to experience. That is why the process for so many is called quieting the mind.

In reality, it is the process of unfocusing, because saying that you are in a process of unfocusing means immediately softening up the sharpness of your mind, and it has a quiet mind as a consequence, not as a destination.

I never really understood what the meaning of ego is. Now I am thinking that what people refer to as ego is actually the mind, the intellectual mind?

It refers to and it is about all of your physicality.

It is you holding on to the identity of your physicality that is called ego. Very important for your survival, very important for you to nurture your body, very important for you to make decisions, but not all of your experience. It is you from a Wider Perspective that is expressing through your ego, and not the other way around.

In other words, you do not want to get rid of the ego, as you are not trying to get rid of your physical focus, you are looking to balance it out. *To find its use at the right time.*

You are looking to allow yourself to have infinite egos when it comes to infinite identities that you are taking on throughout each and every day. Not holding on to one or few of them only. Not holding on to any of them, but gracefully dancing between them.

You really want to dance.

I have heard something that Abraham Hicks has said that really resonates with me – that the subconscious mind becomes conscious when you bring it into your awareness. I am curious to have more clarity of what is a conscious, and what a subconscious mind?

Instead of thinking about all of these levels of the mind, conscious or subconscious, you can look at it from the perspective of memory.

Memory of everything that has been before you comes with your body. And you continue adding to it as you go about your physical experience. Predominantly you are busy experiencing your own memory gathered through your sensory system. And then sometimes, you engage into some generational contexts which are all imprinted in your DNA.

That is often where you are thrown off and you feel as if something that you have no control over is running your life experience.

Then comes the time where you cannot take that anymore and want to experience it from a different perspective. And with any tools available to you, you find steadiness by creating a little bit of a distance between that which is you and your memory.

You are your memory for as long as *you* give attention to it.

Once you understand that you are the one directing your attention, either to the memory, or to the now or to the future, you are not consumed and overwhelmed by it because you are not attaching yourself, trying to hold on to it. You simply have the access.

So it is not about erasing any or all of the memories. You keep getting and making them, keep having access to all the contexts of all the memories, of all the history of you, your family, your society, the world at large, and Everything That Exists that you have access to.

Whether it keeps being gathered by you or you dive into the generational memory, *you have access to it, but you are not it.*

This is a powerful stance to be. To be able to look into any materialized memory, and not be thrown off by it, regardless of your preference. *This is what it means to be conscious.*

> ***I have sensations and emotions that during my childhood I was happy and it was beautiful. But I do not have many memories about it. Why?***

Because you are either in the place of now, not having access to any of the memory, or you are looking ahead, or some other memory from the past is more dominant within you. Sometimes it can be because some experience was more favorable than the other. This is about you making preferences, and of course choosing the ones that feel better rather than the others, and often covering up the ones that do not feel good.

Once you get so good at practicing the process of unfocusing and getting to the perspective of beyond thought, you then see that you can dance around, not only through the memory of what you have added within this physical experience, but also through the ones that were formed before this physical iteration.

This is how you can resolve, within you, all of the conflict that has ever been. Many refer to it as collective energy cleaning, cleansing or generational healing. Once you set yourself consistently in your wider stance, you become this vessel for spreading the light. That means you go ahead and anything you give your attention to has a potential to become wonderful. When you witness the ones being steady within themselves, and capable of taking on tasks that seem inhuman to you and others, this is what they are doing. They have found the tool, they are applying the tool, and now it is not sufficient for them for that tool to be only within them.

They cannot but include more and share that light with anyone who is looking for their next step towards finding consistency in awareness of their own light.

> ***I know we can access the history of everything. But can we access the future? And can you predict the future or see the future?***

There are certain tendencies that can be witnessed from a Wider Perspective when you step back. Through your sense of steadiness, you can see where the people or bigger groups around you are in their evolution.

Based upon that, you can predict the trends. Whether those trends are going to stay on the level of potentiality or actually fulfill does not depend on you. But you can see the tendencies and you can anticipate the tendencies based on your steady observation.

Witnessing the tendencies of someone is being asked to reflect to them where they are at the moment. People asking for predictions are really asking for a reflection of what their current position is, as a starting point for the next step in their discovery.

> ***I am not sure if I have any other questions about the mind, unless you want to add something else.***

Your mind is your survival tool, but it is also *the doorway* to your Wider Perspective. And so that is why the balance with the body, for you to experience from that Inner Self perspective, is so important and makes for your biggest desire.

Mind is the most active tool that you have going on in these times. It has always wanted to evolve to these heights, and wants to continue evolving to provide you with more solutions. It also wants to sometimes take a break, so you can see things from a Wider Perspective. So you can bring more of that mutual feedback for your mind to continue to develop, and be of use to you and to all the new and future generations.

It is the most brilliant tool, but it is not you.

CHAPTER FIVE

YOU AND THE OTHERS

Without relationships, you would cease to exist.

In a Wider Perspective, everything represents a relationship for you. Everything you can sense and receive feedback from is in a relationship with you, whether it is a person, animal, nature or an inanimate object. Everything that you perceive through your flashlight of attention is always providing you with reflection. That feedback is in the essence of the relationships and it allows you to see things from a different perspective, and therefore formulate more questions.

In a more specific, practical way, your relationships are predominantly with people.

Different layers of relationships are based on how long, or how often, you have been giving attention to that person. Some relationships are more intense, some more lighthearted, some of them more frequent in exchange, some less consistent in providing feedback, but *all of them are relevant to you, all of them are important to you,* as they all provide you with valuable feedback.

Those relationships that are close, important to you, that define some of your beginning contexts in this physical iteration, are there to provide you with *consistent* mirror reflection of your growth in expression. Your relationships such as with your family members, your life partners, your friends, being those that you give the most attention to, even though you are not necessarily always communicating with them.

While it might appear that all or most of your family relationships are given to you, especially when they pose as such stubborn mirror reflections, *you have chosen these relationships with* even more ease than when you choose your life partner, or your friends. *This is because you are never looking at the feedback to be that which you already see from within.* You are looking for a different angle of expression of that which is within you, to reflect back to you, and stimulate new discoveries within you.

This process is what makes all of your discoveries eternal in nature. Therefore, all of your relationships are eternal in nature, too.

In the consistency of those important relationships, you get to experience continuity of your own development. You utilize that opportunity and use it as a measuring point of your growth—as a marker, as an opportunity to see the brilliance of the eternity that you are a part of.

Therefore, all of your relationships can be looked at from two angles.

There are those people that you interact with, and expect in interacting and communicating with them to get you to the position of steady. To be that steady space for you to move from question to answer. To be that steady energy for you to move, and soften up your focus into the process of unfocusing.

And then there are the ones that stimulate you to ask those questions. Those are the relationships you give attention to, from the place of steady, in the process of formulating the questions. Those are the ones different from you. So different that you get to the position of steady and then observe. Then, because of those differences, you measure and compare and they give you the thrill of new discoveries, even when sometimes the process of observing throws you off balance in your question-answer dance.

These feedbacks, coming through you as a reflection, from everything and anything you give your attention to, are always in their nature either reflecting back to you what you already see from within, or starting the new discovery, for you to experience exactly that – *new layers of you,* as you look within.

You choose your family members, as much as they choose you.

It is a mutual choice of coming in and finding a suitable environment for this physical iteration part of your eternal discovery. It might not always appear that way, especially when the circumstance gets you to an extreme situation of unpleasantness and discomfort. But at all times, while not choosing the details of the situation and circumstance, you choose the opportunity for a new growth sprout.

Everything that has been lived before is a part of you, not only through your family, but through society and through humanity at large. That broad context is embodied within your DNA, and then enhanced through the stories that you are receiving and keep telling.

In the early days of being part of a family and community, part of the group, involved while spending time together, that initial context you are born into is dominant. As you start learning about your physical focus, and how to choose where to give your attention, and how to deliberately switch the attention from one topic to another, not only do you accept the contexts you are a part of, but within them, you start shaping them into your own context of living, too.

While you are in the process of sharpening the pointing of your attention, you commence understanding that where you direct it is your choice at all times. It takes a moment to realize and master this, so most of the time you experience the strengthening of the context you were born into, and sometimes you even consider accepting it in its totality as yours, too.

As you move around and get curious, you explore more and start experiencing something different from your family context. You start shifting it and molding it into that which will become your own mix of inherited and discovered aspects of experience. Never the same for a long period of time, as you are constantly changing and evolving and growing in your discovery. *But sufficiently for you to be able to call it your own.*

You start seeing what parts of that initial context you want to keep, which part you would like to change, and you start embarking on that which is your own journey of choosing your circumstance in a more specific way. *Therefore, that initial context of your family bonds is, and will always be there as the most consistent reflection.* A feedback on what you decided to keep, rather by choice or consistent attention, and what you have done differently in your experience, so the mix of it all becomes that which you are at that moment.

Those important relationships that know you so well, that know who you were, often point you back to that perspective of what *it was.* They often remember you in a specific past position of your own growth. And while too much of that measurement and comparison can sometimes throw you off, it is always valuable for you to experience it, as it is the opportunity for you to be more inclusive.

More inclusion of all versions of you, that have been, are now, and will continue to be.

For you are not simply shedding all of those experiences from before. You are shifting, you are including more of the layers of you. Then you have the choice in your practice of unfocusing to dip into all of those memories and contexts that were dominating your experience for some time, in the amount of your own choosing.

No matter the circumstance, you never really want to fully take out all the aspects of your original early context of your family. There are always behaviors and memories that are suitable for you to keep. For as long as you see that *your initial family context is just a springboard for your discovery,* you keep the power, the reins of your creation process in your own hands.

Your family relationships are some of the most intense ones you can experience. Intense in experiencing love, but also a discomfort when the variety is observed for too long. Therefore, you often find that inclusivity first with your friends. Then life partners. Then with all of your family members. Including more and eventually all versions of contexts of your becoming, and seeing it as a valuable feedback that you can check in with as often and as long as you want to, is what keeps your journey eternal.

These stubborn mirrors reflecting back to you are often the last ones you deliberately include in your flashlight of attention, and it comes with growth in consistency of spending time in your Wider Perspective and experiencing your human potential.

So, be easy with them as it is natural for those stubborn, sometimes stuck-feeling contexts to take a moment to be molded, and shifted, and accessed through the power of your will.

How does the mirror reflection happen? For example, how do two people reflect to each other different angles of themselves. What is the process, and why is it coming specifically from a certain person? Is it about the Law of Attraction, where your energy must match the energies of the other person, and then they reflect to each other?

It happens at all times, but you become aware of it only when you are ready to experience the new dimensions of you.

In certain moments, the Self is the predominant stance you are standing in. While you are seeing yourself as separate from others, you witness them doing things to you, whether positive or negative, but you do not see it as a reflection of you. At that moment of experiencing the shape of your definition, the boundary of you to its fullest, you want more, because you are now predominantly in a question from the position of separation.

In the moments of having softer physical senses, you start discovering that you are not Self only, that you are Oneness embodied in Self.

Little by little you become aware that if *you are One* embodied in Self, then *others are One* embodied in Self, too, and that there is a common thread that connects everything and everyone. Then you start listening to see where that common thread is, and commence softening your attention outwards more consistently so you can be on a lookout for it more often.

Being in that process of discovery with a certain frequency opens you up to some evidence that *what you observe in your surroundings is a reflection of you*. That common thread might not be seen, but it is sensed, and the moment you start witnessing one evidence after another, one feedback after another, you start experiencing from a perspective where it always happens from—your position of being the light behind the lenses, expressing through all of the physical faculties that are available to you.

As one expresses through the lenses of person A, person B is receiving that through their physical lenses. Now, person B can experience that as a lens and see it as someone else's doing, but they can also experience it as light behind the lens and see it as a reflection of their own doing. For it is having the lens being shined on from a different perspective, and therefore receiving different awareness that could never be received from the angle of Self.

You cannot observe your lenses from the outside, you can observe your lenses only from the inside. And so that which is from the outside comes through other people's lenses. That which is the feedback of more *One* for you comes from other people's lenses.

When you include even further, when you start understanding that We All Are One, that everything is One, you see *that you are placing those experiences from a Wider Perspective, and you want to witness them from different angles. You want to have access not only to yours, but to all the angles.*

This is the essence of your eagerness for more and what gives birth to all your desires. This is what makes you dissatisfied with only your own angle, your own perspective, from where you stand at the moment.

The more consistently you perceive from the Wider Perspective, the more you see that Everything That Exists makes up 99.9999999% of that common thread and that 0.0000001% makes for the wonderfulness of your physicality, through the perspective of focus as you know it. This minor percentage triggers so much discovery of that which is majorly you, which is divinity, expressing through physicality.

And so you want to see more of that which you are, you want to express more of that which is your light. This is why many refer to it as an enlightenment, because you want to see and experience more of that light. And the only way to do that through your physicality is to have more inclusiveness and to have access to more light bulbs.

In other words, you do not want to perceive it only from one angle, you do not want to witness it only partially, to flow only one ray of light. You want to experience as much of it as you can, you want to experience it all. And to do that, through the lenses of your physicality, you want some assistance in the form of having multiple, numerous mirrors through others' lenses, reflecting back to you.

You want everyone's light bulbs to turn on as well.

You want to be that inclusive and steady to see that others are you from the position of one, and to have that wholeness reflecting back to you, in your position of Self, through the lenses of others.

Do you sometimes witness the shadow and predominantly light, or the other way around, or anything in between? That is really the only work you are ever interested in doing.

When there is someone who is doing something negative, and there is someone that is receiving that negative, how does that work? Are they both a reflection of each other?

So, an action of one has caused the reflection of negative emotion within the other one. Here are some possibilities to consider.

One or both could be in the perspective of Self predominantly, and then having that matching, mutual experience.

One can be predominantly in the perspective of Self, and the other one perceives it as a reflection and knows that there is value in it, even though they do not see that value at the moment of receiving that negative reflection.

One or both of them could be seeing this experience as a mutual reflection, and therefore shift happens rather quickly because both are aware that there is a value. Therefore, because there is a value, even though they do not see it, they do not make a big deal out of the negativity part of it, but they pull to the Wider Perspective sooner, knowing that the reflection will provide clarity at some point and they will know what the value for it is along the way.

One or both can be in the position of such inclusiveness and deliberately expressing from a Wider Perspective, knowing that they were looking for that trouble and actually looking to have that experience for themselves, so they can see their light more inclusively.

Following these examples, there are more possibilities that can be there. Ultimately, it is not that only the ones that are experiencing from predominantly Self are only interacting with the ones predominantly Self, even though that is often the case. But a variety of people, based upon where they are in their discovery of who they really are, interacting with each other and matching up.

Everyone has their own experience. So one can have the experience of Self and one can have the experience of one, even though they are having the mutual conversation, or interaction, or the experience.

In other words, one can be causing a negative experience, or doing something wrong to someone from the perspective of Self, bringing discomfort, competition, too much measurement and comparison, insecurity. And the other one can see that totally from the perspective of "I have opened the door to look for some trouble, and here it is. Let me see how quickly I can include the value of even this experience, as it can turn into me seeing more of my life through that lens."

So, what about the cases when someone is raping someone. How does that work as a mirror reflection?

At that moment there is no reflection, there is only an experience between two perspectives of Self.

Those unfortunate situations do happen, even though they are not necessary for either of the participants. Also, they are heavier on the participant who is doing the negative deed than they are on the one who is receiving it. They bear more weight in their own discovery of feeling of freedom and liberation, than the one receiving the trouble at that moment.

While you do not choose all the circumstances at all times, you always choose the discovery path.

So why does that happen? What do you mean by there is no reflection at that moment?

The person giving that negative experience would never do it if there was an opportunity for that person to have the reflection about it. But in a perspective of such dense separation of Self, as in the example you described, there is no wholeness experienced on either side.

In other words, if either of the participants could be in a Wider Perspective to have the awareness that there can be such a negative experience like this, they would never choose such an extreme negative feeling.

They would choose curiosity to formulate the question, and not these really extreme negative experiences. And so, there is the one giving that pain from the place of Self and the other one receiving pain from the place of Self, and that is why we say there is no reflection going on at the moment. There is mutuality, there is attention, there is that which is growth, but there is no awareness of that being a reflection, because the perceiving at the moment is in an extreme position of Self.

The possibility of movement from being predominantly focused on Self into having something as a reflection, and then moving into the wholeness with everything and everyone, is faster for the person receiving than for the one that is orchestrating that kind of a tremendously negative experience.

So, how does that mutuality happen? What is mutuality?

It happens through your attention and choices you make in situations that stimulate your growth.

It is understandable that it can be hard to imagine that anyone would ever specifically choose something like a process of rape, and it is true that no one does.

But the process of the evolutional sprout is really determined by you and everyone else for themselves. It is your opportunity to move to more awareness of that which you really are, which is that everything you give attention to is a reflection of you, and furthermore, it is you from a different angle.

Full inclusivity moves you into living that full-fledged human experience and your journey, not all the details of it, but the journey on its own, is always your choice.

Because you are always looking, in every physical iteration, to peel off more of physical focus outwards and move on towards understanding the Oneness that you are, the wholeness that you are, expressed through your physicality.

What do you mean by different angles?

It is like a mirror.

While you are not looking at it, you have one awareness of you, and then you put one mirror in front of you, and you move into a different awareness of you because of that new angle.

Your original mirrors are your parents, a child, or a family member important to you. As you grow up, you start adding the layers of your acquaintances, friends, life and business partners. When you feel in harmony with all these relationships, you then want to stretch that circle and include everyone and anyone you interact with, or even further, everyone you give attention to, to represent that different angle of you.

Not everyone is ready to have an experience so inclusive and witness others from different angles in their current physical iteration. Some are moving from the Self-perspective to the reflection layer, some from the reflection to various angles, and some gallop through the layers within one lifetime. But *everyone is always within the full range* of living this all-inclusive potential.

So, the ones that find their own steadiness are eager to keep having more reflections than the ones that are still looking for tools that will get them to be there consistently. They are ready to spice it up, even knowing the reflections will sometimes make them feel overwhelmed.

They are looking for more of that movement, motion forward that brings them to express more and more from the perspective of who they really are.

> ***How do you define eternal discovery? Even though we are mostly unfocused when we are born, we come with different intentions. Why do we do that? To expand the non-physical?***

What you are really asking for is about the purpose. You are asking about your eternal destiny.

You do not work for anyone else but for you. It is all the choice based upon where you point your flashlight of attention. *You have the choice at all times.* There is no one outside of you leading the way, other than you. Even asking if your job is to develop or to grow the non-physical points towards the separateness from that which is non-physical, which cannot be.

You are doing that for you. It is very selfish in nature, that which is your growth and experience. Selfish to get to a position of steady, and then expressing selflessness as application of your steady.

In other words, *it is all you, for you.* And then everyone else benefits from that, too.

So, what is the meaning of eternal discovery?

If there was a destination, how would that experience feel to you? If there was an expiration date? How would that feel to you? If there was an end to the story? How would that feel to you?

With all the feedback you are receiving at all times, from anything and everyone you are giving attention to, you want to experience more. More of that eternal question-answer dance that so many can describe in such different ways.

But who would not want to dance eternally? Who would not want to ask and receive eternally?

Who would not want to witness more of that which is a reflection back, so there is more divinity and bliss to be expressed and experienced?

I am curious about what you mentioned before, that there is always a mutuality in choosing our families. Our family chooses us and we choose them. What about families where parents are not really biological parents to their children.

The process of getting focused in the body is a specific choice.

Therefore, the one who will be the stubbornest mirror reflection, and the one who will be the carrier of that which is the transformation from physical unfocus to focus, do not have to be the same.

That which is the family bond and parenting has less to do with physicality, and more with involvement and inclusivity.

Often that biological part is strong within you, but the variety of observing sometimes causes different situations to lead you to different outcomes. The reflections that are put in front of you are always equally proportional to the amount of variety you are matching with and are capable of observing. First the variety you want to commence with at your birth, and then the variety that you want to continue including yourself into.

Those circumstances are sometimes there for you to have the experience of question-question ping-pong which feels like you are hitting your head against the wall, but eventually you shift that back to balance. Sometimes you need to shake things up with some extra focus to move your flashlight of attention the other way around in a more drastic fashion. And sometimes, that is not necessary.

This is always, at all times, your choice, knowing you can be predominantly balanced and still feel the thrill and speed of your creation from that steady position.

How does the choice to be born happen? How does the Wider Perspective with no physical faculties, make choices to come and focus again into physicality?

The integration of that which is physical and non-physical is inseparable. Therefore, there is a rather short period of time in between your physical iterations.

You are constantly looking for a newer, fresher perspective for you to experience and express, every moment of every day while physically focused. And it happens in the same fashion between physical iterations, so you are usually eager to take a new form rather quickly.

To take a new perspective, to take a new angle, all based on all of your cumulative experiences in that and all previous physical iterations.

Why specifically do we want to have life partner?

As you predominantly think of family as something you have been born into, it takes a moment for you to shift away from that context, and realize that you have made those same choices, too.

To get there with your family, you start practicing your deliberate choice making first with your friends. They are of your choosing, and therefore you have the best opportunity to start seeing someone outside of you as a reflection of you. When you get enough evidence that both positive and negative reflections are valuable to you by interacting with your friends, and that you have control over how to respond to these reflections, you are ready to have an even more consistent reflection in the form of a life partner.

With a little bit of time and awareness, you see that both friendships and life partner relationships are no different than the ones you have with your family.

Reflections have always been your choice, and continue to always be valuable to you. They always bring something new – either to shift you towards the answer from the position of question, or to apply that feeling of answer to the discovery of a new question.

All. Always. Valuable. To. You.

Therefore, a life partner is not someone you choose only to reflect the resonance of who you are back to you, but also to reflect a bit of trouble once in a while, so you are inspired to look within even further and discover new layers of that which is your eternal nature.

It is someone like the family, someone you choose deliberately, consciously, to bring you not only the experience of more ease compared to your family balance, but also to get you to experience your day to day inner growth sprout.

Your life partner is the pebble you are putting in your shoe yourself, a most deliberately chosen stubborn mirror that is not easy to ignore, so it is becomes one of your best teachers.

The relationships that are easy to dissolve do not give you all the necessary reflections. The ones you commit yourself to bring you more consistency of variety, which gets you to look within more often. It is in your nature to exist due to having feedback, and the most consistent feedback you can get is with the ones you give most air time in your mind. And while any relationship can become that for you, life partner is the most deliberate choice of a stubborn mirror you can make.

Your life partner is at all times, based on the dominant context that you have at that moment. That person is a mirror reflection of you, and you are a mirror reflection of that person. And since this is the person you give the most of your attention to, it becomes your most consistent reflection that provides you with an opportunity to really bring more inclusiveness into your perspective.

More inclusiveness of others' perspectives of Self, so you can see that Oneness perspective reflected back to you with more clarity.

Undeniable, undoubted awareness of the light you are reflecting back to yourself, from anyone and everything you give your attention to, regardless of where they might be in their discovery.

How would you describe, from the Wider Perspective, the relationship between parents and their children?

You come from the perspective of pure physical unfocus, and with time learn how to focus and you build the context and then you go about it.

And when you are ready to sprout, you invite this new stubborn mirror reflection, your life partner in crime, in terms of your troublemaking to each other. Witnessing not only the positive, but the value of all the reflections you provide to each other, you spring to the next layer of awareness and desire to experience even more inclusiveness.

When you are aware that you can choose to get away from your friends, family, or even from your life partner at any time, but you know the value of that mutual troublemaking and accept it, then you are ready for more inclusion. Then you are ready to include children, too.

Because there is really no looking away from someone you are bringing into this world, as you will be taking care of them at all times, and have them within the flashlight of your attention for the rest of your physical iteration.

And so that which might be felt as a responsibility is you wanting to include more.

You want to observe that which is the sprout of life, building the balance between the process of focusing and unfocusing. That mirror reflection is usually your best teacher, because it allows you to take another shot at witnessing this focus-unfocus, question-answer dance from this developed place, from a perspective of you from a different angle.

Because you cannot not pay attention to your children.

Thank you. I have no questions at this moment. Unless you want to add something else.

Your friends are usually the first ones that you feel can assist you to balance out all the other relationships.

Your family members, life partner and children are consistent reflections providing you with stubborn feedback. In the moments of intensity, you start looking to spend time with someone that will put you in a place of ease, that will put you in a place of getting to witness the value of the process of unfocusing.

You look for someone you can just be with, someone that you do not have to explain anything to. Someone with whom you do not want to stir the pot regarding any of the questions that have been piling up within you so much, or someone that will also take the edge off while spending time together.

When you know that there are other outcomes in relationships but intensity, you look for tools to get you to steady and you get a hold of this focus-unfocus dance. Then your friends start becoming family, and you commence including more of them, not only to have them as a reflection to get to steady, but also to bring them to clarify so many more questions, and therefore initiate more of their discovery.

You are usually light hearted about your friendships, when other relationships are causing you to ask more questions. But once you get a hold of this question-answer dance, you do not even measure things that way, as everything becomes so joyful and wonderful for you that everyone is an opportunity for more of that feedback that you are looking for, in terms of your expansion. And there is also the blissful satisfaction that you feel every step of the way.

CHAPTER SIX

YOU IN THE WORLD

With more clarity about the creation process and details of how it applies to you, and how it is interpreted in your relationship to others – it is time for you to see how you can put this in a context of your showing up in the world, often measured by the feeling of success.

That which is outside of you is predominantly stimulating, and therefore motivating in nature. Witnessing the margins of success of others, you can take some of them as yours, and have them as a part of your own success context. And while it can cause an inspired action within you, it is, at all times, only the beginning position of you realizing the feeling of success within you.

By observing and choosing you got the clarity of wanting, and then released it into discovery. When you are no longer holding it in your image, you can look elsewhere and witness the next steps that have been ready for you since the moment you asked. For you to experience that which once was a question and turned into a desire, into a received idea, and is now turning into an expression of that idea, for you to discover and experience with your physical senses in reality, too

Often, success is perceived as a goal. Often, success is connected with destination. Linked to attaining a platform to be on, a moment in time to reach, a target to hit.

And we want to guide you in a different direction of seeing *success as a process.*

For when you are aware of what the creation process is, and you get a hold of deliberately moving your flashlight of attention from one moment to another, in that kind of creation process, *everything feels like success.*

You have the ability for your feeling of success to be present moment after moment, and for it to come from that place of satisfaction, while navigating your flashlight of attention in your creation process wherever and however long you choose to. This is what generates the feeling of success within you.

At all times, success is an internal process, not an external measurement.

The feeling of success grows and subsidies based on your balance between your focus and unfocus. Between your attention to the question building and to receiving the answers. In that balance, there is a sensation of success.

Since your desires are, and will continue to be created eternally, since your clarity of wanting will be based on eternal preference making, no matter what feeling of achievement happens in any idea that you see come through life, there will always be the next, and the next, and the next, and the next expression you will want to find its way into physicality.

Your feeling of success does not need to be connected only with the moment of physical realization of that idea for which you got the clarity of wanting. You can feel success in every moment while it is in the process of coming through. In other words, you do not need to be limited to feeling success in asking questions and receiving answers only, but you can be free to feel it in every moment in between.

You have the ability to lead a more fluid dance between the question and the answer, as well as between the answer and the question. This way, you allow yourself to witness and open up so many more gift boxes of thrill and satisfaction and success along the way of that which is the physical materialization of the desire you are looking to experience. In conventional business terms, most often it is increased income, promotion in organizations, and wanting to have your own business that represents your success.

You never really succeed at only one thing at a time. There are so many topics you give attention to day in and day out. So many different avenues to which you can apply this beautiful process. So, you can either feel successful or not, and that feeling will trickle down to anything and everything you bring into your awareness.

I would like to get your insights on money. What is money?

This varies based on where you are predominantly in your discovery.

Where you are in your own question-answer dance, when it comes to how often you spend time in giving attention outwards, to measurement, to comparing. Money can represent a goal, something you want to achieve and then attain, a destination of some kind.

You can also see money for what it really is, a tool. Not only for exchange, but a tool that can help you both move from question to answer and from answer to question. Like anything else that you observe in your physicality, money also wants to always be on the move. In other words, it is constantly looking for an expression based on what it is dedicated to.

Therefore, your balance between outward measurement and integration of it within you, that balance really determines what money represents to you.

For the ones observing predominantly from the perspective of Self, there is so much measurement. Therefore, for the most part, money represents the most universal and accepted tool they can rely on for comparison. They focus on money, regardless of whether it brings them steadiness or not.

The ones witnessing others as a reflection of themselves still have that aspect, but use it in a more balanced way. They use it as a tool to get them into their flow because they understand that comparison with others is valuable, but only as the starting point in the whole creation process. They use money as a tool to get steady.

And then there are the ones who get to the perspective of even wider inclusion and integration, seeing that money is like any other thing, person or situation – always a different angle of their own doing, regardless of how good or not good it feels. They encompass it all, seeing the value quicker and moving on to have a more integrated experience. Having attention on money or not does not make a difference to their steadiness. So, if they choose to, it can flow with no limits as it is not detrimental to their experience.

There is always going to be measurement involved, even when you are as inclusive as you can be, as you always measure while still physically focused. How predominant that measurement is within you will determine how long you stay there, and whether it will predominantly represent a destination, or a tool for expression.

> ***If I want to buy a house, I need X amount of money. If I do not have it in my bank account at this moment, how can I get that amount more quickly, so I can buy the house?***

What is the rush for the quicker receiving of the house?

The way you posed the question is from the perspective of destination. The house being a destination. Adding the speed to the current position of measuring, which is not having money, makes for a recipe for trouble. Unless you see this situation only as the starting point of the process that will yield you the receiving of the house.

So, you have a choice.

To continue to measure how much money you need, what goes in the process of obtaining the house, how quickly you want to have it. And therefore, delay the experience of discovering yourself in this house and moving into a position to include money you currently do not have for that house.

Or you can start seeing that this is just a starting point and that money is only a tool for the transaction part of having this house. That softens your attention and instead of going outwards it can now land in a different position. What is this house for? Who is it for? Why do you want to use it?

By asking questions like this, you shift your attention from measuring and you make *the process of receiving a house active.* The moment the process of acquiring is predominant, and you get there by not revisiting the destination aspect of this desire often, all the "hows" and "whens" will be realized by you. And the money will flow.

The best thing that can happen is if you could get the clarity of the wanting firmed up with a few of the "whys." This way, you make sure you are not back to the observe-choose part of the creation process. You are not looking at the gap between the money you have and what you need to get a house.

And once it is firmed up, you revisit *it only once in a while* and only when you feel super steady. You do anything necessary to have the balance between your ongoing questions and the answers. So you can release even the "Whys."

Then those avenues for you to take will be crystal clear to you. They have always been there; you just didn't see them until you were ready. You can never see them and listen to them and experience them if you are in that position of the starting point for too long.

You cannot experience the desire and its fulfillment at the same time, so the vision of the house has to give, in order for you to move into it.

So, I do not even have to think about the money itself?

Since money still represents the measurement for so many, it is natural to have it in the awareness, as you are consistently observing variety, and therefore gathering insights. When money is in the position of measuring, it only ignites the starting point of your discovery.

When you become aware that measuring did its purpose, you can then soften that aspect of money and start engaging with its tool aspect, which is a mechanism for exchange. This is when you are ready *to be one with the process and not the destination.*

You can switch your perspective on money by using any tool you know to get you to the perspective of steady. *The sooner you can move from measuring to using the tool for steady, the sooner the money starts showing up as a tool for exchange, rather than measurement.* In other words, it starts flowing into your experience so you can spend it where you desired to begin with.

You cannot continue to measure, and measure, and measure, and measure and expect it to come into your experience. The process of integration is moving your flashlight of attention from measurement to answer, from asking more questions to finding the steady, from asking more questions to finding ease and relaxation.

Especially if it is a big desire, measurement takes quite a lot of your focus. So, you want to find more balance within that. Ideally, you see money as a measurement, as a destination, as a goal only at the starting point of your motivation, and then you get yourself into steadiness as soon as you can. You do that by using the tools to get you as unfocused as you can be.

When you continue revisiting that topic, only from the position of steady, you speed things up. When you revisit that topic, or that goal from the position of question, you delay its manifestation.

For you cannot receive while you are measuring.

How do people become multimillionaires or even billionaires?

For some, *measurement is important.* For those whose perception is predominantly from the perspective of Self. They use it, as well as money, as a destination and when they do, their ride is usually rocky.

They are asking question after question after question after question after question and then rapidly, quickly releasing the whole pile of them and receiving big downloads. Then again, piling up question after question after question after question after question, followed by quick release, and then a lot of flow coming through. These are rather spiky experiences and not smooth, exhilarating rides. That is why you witness so many people having so many successful projects with a lot of money as an outcome, and then losing them at some other time. Some even go through it times and times again.

And then you have those who have similar experiences of receiving the money, but then they flow it together with all of desires along the way. In other words, money is the means for them, only a *tool to be living their desires.*

You see this with the pioneers. You see this with scientists. You see this with visionaries, the ones that have been dancing with this question-answer dance, observing so powerfully with their senses, and then pulling out into the Wider Perspective and seeing the potential of humanity unfolding for years, dozens of years, hundreds of years ahead.

Then, there are the ones who find it easy to balance between focus and unfocus. They measure and then they ease up to receive their idea. They compare and then they relax to receive inspiration. They ask and then they soften up to receive the answer that will lead their next action steps.

Their ongoing individual experience is based on balance.

It is safe to say that what you are dreaming up is stimulated by your observing. Looking around and comparing does not have to be a negative experience, it does not have to be troublesome. Even though survival ignites the fire within you, and you often bring it to your non-survival desires, most of your experiences do not have to be experienced by you in that manner.

You can predominantly be present in your *happily ever now.* You can observe something, measure it, unfocus, see it flowing through, experience it, observe again, measure it. It can be as easy to have your ideas be received in and expressed out, in and out, smoothly and comfortably.

Some are keeping money as a sort of security, because they have fears developed that they need to have it to feel safe, or they believe that they need to provide for others. They do not believe that others are capable.

Some have piled up money with so much attention to the measurement to others, that their experience is everything but satisfying.

And then there are the ones flowing abundance in and out, smoothly flowing it through.

Those are the ones that you see that are moving your world in the direction of more ease and satisfaction and new ideas for betterment. They are developing those ideas in order to push their and the experience of others, of all humanity, into a better feeling place. There is so much evidence available for you to witness this. And while there will always be observing of variety and experiencing differences for the majority of people, the circumstances of living are exponentially improving.

It might be hard to sometimes see, but everyone, at all times, no matter how their intentions feel to you, even the ones who seem to have been piling up money for measurement and for their own good only, all of them are essentially flowing Everything That Exists within the Wider Perspective, and applying it into physicality for the good of everyone else to the best of their ability.

It is just that some of them get stuck in the measurement a little longer by bringing survival mode where it does not belong and where it does not have to be. And some have been more balanced in their creation, and are reflecting back to you their and everyone else's natural intention more clearly.

If someone is born in a place where there is predominantly a perception of scarcity around money, how does that person shift their perception to experience more abundance?

They either start softening the attention towards what is happening and start finding the balance or they intensify the attention into that scarcity until it cannot be handled anymore, so the shift happens.

It can be a more gradual process. This is always recommended, always suggested as that is what you came to predominantly experience – to find the balance, like every particle in the Universe. But it is also based on an outward stimulation, on individual's journey and sensitivity to the environment.

Sometimes that which is perceived as scarcity and fear can be so predominantly active, that numbing the experience and trying to seclude through whatever tools of numbing are available can be the first step for it. Since *the fear is an exaggerated question,* the balance during that brief relief is rather quick, and it stops serving its purpose swiftly because you have not got there deliberately.

Since you could not have directed yourself away from the questions, you are back to intensifying them by giving them more spotlight. As the reins of your attention are not in your hands to choose otherwise. During this constant asking there comes the moment where you cannot add more discomfort to your experience and you tip the point in the direction of unfocusing.

At some point you cannot but try to feel better. Then you are on a quest on how to get there, and the tools start unveiling themselves to you.

I got into the awareness that while there are different topics, and it is beneficial to speak about a variety of them, I feel like there is one answer to all of them – which is the balance between focus and unfocus. If I have a question, to receive the answer I use any tool to successfully unfocus. Once I receive the answer, I gently apply my unfocused

perspective into the discovery of the next question, the curiosity of it. I feel that each and every one of us is really asking for the balance in experiencing their question-answer dance.

Everyone, at all times, as every particle in the Universe, is looking to find the balance and move things around and then find the new balance, and then repeat that again, and again, and again as the feeling of balance is never about one and the same balance you catch and hold on to forever.

It is always, for everyone, about the process of balancing.

You are always finding a new balance, because from a different perspective of too much focus or too much unfocus, you feel either overwhelmed by action or stuck without taking any.

When you are predominantly experiencing oversaturated amounts of focus, and you need to unfocus to regain the balance between your body, mind, thoughts and emotions, you start paying closer attention to how much air time you give outwards. Perceiving from the perspective of Self is a natural part of your evolution, and has never had as much potential as it has now to be shifted towards you seeing that others are a reflection of you.

And therefore, you start moving your focus to the position of some unfocus and then you want to stay there consistently for as long as you want. Which is only the next step, the next layer before you start deliberately deciding how much of that reflection you really want to experience. And how much of that reflection you are ready to witness from your position of steadiness.

At the time when you are the one opening the doors for feedback, you have another tipping point of seeing so much resonance with reflections that you clearly see – everything that has been happening to you has always been you, *as everyone is you from a different angle.*

That is when your all-inclusive party starts.

Since the evidence of what you are observing is predominantly suggesting too much action as materialized focus, it might be hard for you to see, but there are also the ones that are predominantly unfocused, too. They are looking to regain and keep the focus for a longer time on certain topics that are outside of them. Because they have been in that place of Wider Perspective, for a longer time. A lot of new parents, and especially mothers, can be in that position, where they are secluded from usual, everyday interaction with the outside world.

When you feel so unfocused that you feel that you are ready to experience more movement, you want to flow the focus to generate more questions. You have been assured that you can easily access the Wider Perspective on demand, so you are looking for some more trouble on purpose.

Whatever perspective is predominant within you, you are looking for more of the opposite one to balance it out.

And, what about recognition? What is recognition? Why do we seek it?

Recognition is like money, when in the position of measurement.
It is an outside factor, a goal, a sense of achievement, it is something to get to if someone agrees you have done something good. But it is *for you* to achieve something, it is you in the process of achieving something and sometimes having so much attention on the goal of what you are trying to achieve.

That does not mean do not go for promotion, or do not do more, as that is the most natural part of the creation process in your ever-stimulating environment. To start somewhere and then to want to express more, while experiencing progress in those organizational structures that are there for a particular reason. So, there is that experience of using measurement, that starting goal, the achievement to clarify your desire. *But then it is your choice how quickly you get there by balancing your own question-answer dance.*

As with the money, when you observe recognition or promotion as the only identity that matters and you continue to measure it consistently, you keep yourself away from it. Once you see it as a measurement first, and *then switch to looking at it as a tool* to direct you back to the process of the work you are doing, you start setting yourself up for many recognitions along the way.

Recognition is not one moment in time, someone agreeing you are doing a good job.

It is you recognizing it, you promoting, you flowing through your attention with every step of the way while doing what you do. And once you have embodied so much of the process, once you are enjoying it, once you are so thrilled, so engaged with everything that you are giving your attention to, *you cannot not achieve* that which is your next accumulated position, and measure it with satisfaction.

In addition to that, when you are in full involvement like this – everyone wants to be around you. When you are in the position of a consistently engaged life force flowing through you, which is finding expression through your project or a business you are involved with. Now everyone wants to be in on that process. Everyone wants to have that experience, too.

And that's the moment when you are in the position where you can receive recognition and continue to express even more. Money, or recognition, or promotion means you see that this is a measurement, you see that it is only the starting, motivation point in your creation. You are in such a flow of creating, feeling so steady, that you are ready to start receiving feedback.

Not only in the form of a positive reflection. You also want others to provide you with feedback of all kinds. It is okay to sometimes feel a critique reflecting back to you, because without it you cannot get to experience what is next for you to include. How do you know what else to include, if you do not see first what is lacking?

Now, you do not want to, nor do you have to stay there for too long. You stay there long enough to clarify your wanting and then start moving into using that awareness to recognize that the measurement has already done its work, and now it is time for you to move to a perspective of seeing it reflect back to you from reality, rather than from the perspective of desire.

> ***Why do people want to own their own business when even if you work for someone else, it is still your business you are conducting. How would you expand on that and on the idea of having a business?***

There are the ones that do not care about their name being out there.

They do not care about money as measurement. They are looking to flow their light into physicality. They are involved in the process so much, that the ones owning the business witness they are as equally engaged in the business as them, and then adequately reward them with recognition, as well as financial compensation. Because the dance is mutually exciting.

When you are predominantly in Self perspective, you see business owners on the one side and clients on the other side, but both separate from you. You do not see them as you, but as someone that you have to interact with to provide for yourself. And while that is the starting point for everyone, to settle on those basic necessities, you want to observe only food and shelter as something you need, and then everything else as a bonus, as a blessing.

When you are so steady and in the process of creating, when you feel Oneness with someone else's business, you are ready to move on because you want more feedback. You want more reflections pointed back at you. You want more mirrors to engage with so you can express more.

So you take the leap, and there are all these situations that were in the background before, that you were shielded from as you did not have to think about them and you had all the freedom to be giving your attention to the process of creation only.

And now you see that there are so many angles of business that have never been a part of your attention. It was not your business in question, so you did not have to lose sleep over those details, you did not have to figure them out, you did not have to go and get steady so you can see them from a Wider Perspective, because it was beyond your scope of work. *You were not ready for it.*

Even while working for others, you can commence practicing getting inclusive and curious like you own the business you are working for, by wanting to take care of some of those aspects that you have not done before. This is how you get promotion effortlessly. By feeling so balanced with the work in your current position, that you are ready to experience every aspect of business like it is your own. Sooner rather than later, you get to that perspective of knowing that there will always be another angle you can perceive business from, and you get excited about questions and their persistence of showing up and realize that *you will never be able to practice or project every step ahead.*

The difference between you working for someone and you working for yourself is in the preparedness for so many more reflections, because when you work for someone, they are providing that reflection to you. *It takes decisiveness to choose consistency to get to steadiness.* It takes a moment for you to practice it enough so you are ready to be looking for trouble, instead of letting trouble find you.

When everyone is co-creating in an organization or working on a project, and some are unsteady and some are steady, how does that work?

Everyone who is giving attention to a topic, or a project, or a business process is contributing to that process and not only that. They are creating it all, too. Regardless of how big or small their contribution is, each and every person is affecting the creation of the whole thing.

The ones that are steady can see the whole vision, the whole picture. And the ones that are not as steady usually see the segment of that vision. And while they are still creating the whole thing, they are aware of only one aspect at the time, due to their attention to questions being predominant.

In other words, the steady ones are pulling into the Wider Perspective with more ease, and are therefore capable of seeing the whole thing. And the ones that are more predominantly in the perspective of Self, while witnessing a piece of the creation they are working on, they do not see that they are creating everything, too.

Even through their unsteadiness based in exaggerated attention to questions.

They are responsible for it all, but they are not experiencing the whole creation while creating it. Because they are focused in a perspective of Self, they are not pulling into the Wider Perspective, like the ones that are steady.

And so, while everything, and everyone is creating the whole, how much of that whole you are experiencing is up to you. It is up to your focus-unfocus balancing dance, for you to be able to see feedback as a valuable reflection and not a distractive force. So you can see the creation you are working on all-inclusively.

You can pull into a Wider Perspective so much that you can experience the whole Cosmos, the whole Universe, Everything That Exists, at the palm of your hand. You have the ability to access it, and experience it all.

I have the sensation that whatever I feel during the project, is also the energy that I offer to this project and receive the feedback along the way, including the result of it.

The feedback you are receiving is always responding to how many bites of the whole cake you are ready to witness while the cake is baking.

All of the energy is contributing. Small and big, positive and negative.

Sometimes you want to think that you would want to have people working on a project who are only bringing the answers. Yet, someone needs to stir things up. Someone needs to be the troublemaker so the questions can be raised, so the expansion can happen, so the Wider Perspective is considered enough, so attention is turned to the process of unfocusing, so more can be included in your physical experience.

It is equally contributing to the project. Each question that is coming through generates the answer, so there is a great value on both sides, and therefore everyone is creating everything, regardless of how different their experiences in that organization are.

And how would you describe the flow or the process between the client and the service?

Client predominantly asking questions. Service predominantly providing the answers.

Predominantly. Not absolutely.

Service is expected to be more consistent in the position of steady. This gives the clients permission to ask a bigger or more intense number of questions they have been wanting to ask for some time. Pending the steadiness of the service, more can be asked with little to no fear that it will throw them off.

This is what allows clients to receive the answers. The comfortable, steady environment to ask questions.

For that, a steady service is the key. Very much like what you are experiencing now, with all of your potent questions.

Now that you mentioned expectations, what are they? What is the role of expectation within the creation process?

Expectation is really an exaggerated thought, many times recycled and repeated, being impressed through the same pathway over and over again until the flashlight of attention almost automatically goes to that same position of the creation process that matches that thought.

With each impression of the same thought, you make a little dent. When you take the same path, you stay there a bit longer every next time you impress it, so that originally light-hearted thought, easy to be included or not, now becomes more acute, more consistent, more anticipated and turns into its dense version in the form of an expectation.

When you realize that repetition of the impressed thought and its density do not serve you anymore, you commence the process of unfocusing so you can bring it into the lighter form. You use any tool you have to disperse the sharpness of your attention and pull into the Wider Perspective any time, and therefore the topic that includes that densified thought.

Revisiting that topic only from the position of steady gets you to avert density into lightness.

It is important to note that you do not go from one expectation to another in moments in time. That never happens because of the consistency of thought being impressed from the same angle over and over again.

That is where consistency of balancing the question-answer dance kicks in and highlights the importance of the process of unfocusing. So, you look into an expectation from the perspective of steady until you can choose how long you want to stay on it, and how long you want to stay on other topics. You look at it only from a steady perspective until you gain enough confidence by observing enough evidence that it is getting lighter.

This is how you change your past. This is how you shed your karma. *By making a distance so you can observe it, not impress it.* This is how you allow you to be ok with all of your memory.

In other words, you reach a consistency of being in a Wider Perspective, at your terms, so you can go to any memory and not be thrown off by the dent that you made, *because you have ironed it out already.*

CHAPTER SEVEN

FULL-FLEDGED HUMAN BEING

You perceive your physical iteration from the perspective of Self. *But you are not Self only.* Your standpoint of Self is the vessel that allows you to experience all the variety, and express through anything and everything you desire. You are a Divine flow, energy embodied, expressing through an immense amount of variety that is the consequence of consistent feedback that physicality provides.

You come into the physical iteration predominantly soft in your attention outwards, and therefore predominantly aware of who you are. As you start to build the muscle of your physical focus at a young age, you start exploring that balance between being unfocused less and giving attention outwards more. So much variety provides you with a lot of physical stimulation. And that stimulation allows you to sharpen up your flashlight of attention.

Along the way, you may identify yourself so much with your focus on variety, that you feel like that is all there is to your experience. And while you cannot miss being aware of who you are for too long, you are sometimes rather constrained in the experience of your physicality. In other words, that angle which allows you to generate so many questions is dominant. Therefore, you see others as separate from you. You see them *only* as separate from you.

This brings a lot of measurement, comparison, and maybe even the feeling of competition, as your flashlight of attention pointed in your physical focus is designed to do that for you. It allows you to take things apart, then analyze them, and put them back together so you keep yourself safe. It plays the role of maintaining your survival.

But even in that aspect, you are never 100% of your time in the perspective of experiencing only questions and being only outwardly focused. Though maybe not predominantly, you get to the standpoint of some kind of ease or release of focus each day you live. Even if only for a few moments at a time, you relax into less stress by being away from that state of consistent measuring. You live those moments regardless of how you get there – by sleeping, meditating, engaging in a fun activity, or through a certain amount of physical exercise that takes the edge off from your running mind. Everyone gets to that perspective daily.

In the satisfaction of being unfocused for a moment, as you keep coming back to your predominant question-self perspective, you start the shift. You start desiring to experience less of that which is overwhelming, and more of that which is a balance. You start noticing, in glimpses, that Self is not all that makes for who you are. This experience is your shift towards the next layer of your human experience.

The shift is that you still see yourself as Self and others as Selves, but you also start noticing *the common thread* with others. You start recognizing mutuality with your surroundings, and you are able to respond to more of it. You start moving from seeing others as completely separate from you, and you recognize that, while they are in their own perspective of Self, they are also *a reflection of you.* Motivating, or inspiring, either way a reflection of you. You start seeing the value in what feedback others are bringing, and you start celebrating knowing that the beginning stage of any learning process is based on those reflections.

First, you open yourself up to *positive reflections,* as that is a more natural stance, and therefore easier for you to accept. You start witnessing that more and more people are reflecting back to you that positive emotion, ease, satisfaction, confidence, and a truly uplifting state. It starts resonating that this reflection of you through the lens of others is a common thread that somehow connects you with each of them. Therefore, you surround yourself with those who reflect back to you that which is more steadiness.

This brings you to experience more balance between your question and the answer. It gets you to explore more satisfaction than you have ever had before. And it opens the door for you to see that you are connected to everything and everyone that exists around you – other people, animals, nature. You do not only imagine, but you can now sense that common thread moving through. The more of Oneness you tap into, the more of what you want to see shows up in your reality.

As this shift occurs, and enough physical evidence supports it, you are ready to include the next layer of reflections as yours, too. You start seeing that even the *negative reflections* still represent and equally are you.

This layer of awareness is what gives you feedback, not only to recognize the common thread of Oneness in everything and everyone you are observing, but also to allow you to see how the whole creation process works. So you shift and you dance between the question and the answer, using the tools or any positive reflection to get you to the perspective of steady. And once you are there, seeing enough of that Oneness in others, you start seeing that there cannot be separation between you and any kind of feedback that is coming to you.

As it is all perceived by you, all received by you, all integrated by you.

When you take this awareness and turn it into an exercise, a challenge, an exciting tool for you to witness more of Oneness, you start shifting from the need to unfocus only when you feel overstimulated in your focus. You start desiring to increase your steady, so you can look into those reflections on purpose, even though they sometimes occur as troublesome or discomforting.

You feel Oneness and recognize that all positive feelings that reflect your true nature are only consistently growing in its measure because you are giving attention to the variety around you. Because you are getting the feedback that it is not only positive. Because you are getting a variety of feedback, and have an option to choose what you make out of it.

Therefore, you start really embracing this wonderful experience of reflections. *You know, more than before, that everything is your doing.* You know that those predominant experiences of you seeing yourself from the perspective of Self can never be the same to you, as you cannot un-know what you already know. You cannot lock back this new layer of awareness that is coming through you, since it has already been unlocked from within.

And so you keep seeing the value in your unique perspective of Self, but you see more and more value in all of the reflections, too. Knowing that all of these feedbacks and reflections are tools that provide assistance to your discovery, as they are constantly telling you where you are at. They reflect back to you to see in what part of the creation process you are at the moment, so you can be more deliberate and put the reins of your creation back in your own hands.

And you do not stop there.

You keep evolving. When you see the value of Self, you see enough of Oneness reflecting back to you, and then you want more.

You want a full feeling of liberation, a true feeling of freedom. To be in a stance where you predominantly see the Oneness aspect that you have started so joyfully to discover. You start moving towards all-inclusiveness, knowing the value exclusive perspective of Self provides, but also knowing the value of giving attention to reflections from others, so you can have physical experience from a Wider Perspective expressing through all of your physical faculties.

Then you rush to experience some trouble. Then you rush into more of that variety. Then you rush to see what kind of feedback or difference is going to show itself to you, so you can find new layers of ecstasy, thrill, bliss, freedom, ease, and unconditional love.

This wide perspective applied to your physicality does not exclude the other two layers you have been going through before. That is why there are no levels, but perspectives of different aspects, moving and shifting from one to another angle, knowing that all of the layers of your evolution have the value for the rest of this, and in every other physical iteration.

Your desire does not turn into diminishing the Self. It does not become longing to have no reflections back. It does not become a wish for being so detached in a Wider Perspective that you cannot experience physicality.

Your desire becomes *knowing that, at all times, you are making the choice.* You know that you can choose how much time and attention you give to any and every part of the creation process. You become aware of every part of it. You become aware of the feedback mechanism with such a precision, that at all times you see equal value in both aspects of an infinite wave of the question-answer dance that keeps evolving as you do with your experiences.

To have this resonate within you as a potential is a starting point.

Everything else is your choice.

You can find satisfaction in being predominantly in the perspective of Self. You can find satisfaction being more balanced through seeing reflections as yours. But none of that compares to the potential feeling of you in an all-inclusive perspective, from where you see that you are not the lens that you are looking through. That you are not only in your physicality of that body, mind, emotions and thoughts, but rather the light behind those lenses of expression.

And so, it is up to you to choose how much of that potential you want to experience in this physical iteration.

There are no limits to your ability to respond, and therefore experience any layer of eternal expansion within the time frame that you desire. There is no wrong or right path, because your path is *your* discovery. And so you can find satisfaction within it all.

Why is that which is considered positive more natural to us than the negative state?

Because what you are is looking for expression. Because what you are is looking for more of that resonance with the ease, and the bliss, and the stillness, and the light, and the love that you are.

You are embodied in variety to discover more of that which you are.

Therefore, it is an eternal, never ending wave of bliss, blessing, satisfaction, love, and thrill that makes for your most natural stance. And so, stirring things up is all that the negative emotion is for, so you can find and express more of the positive ones.

Are all these positive feelings like love, bliss, appreciation, Divine – static?

It is never the same question asked and therefore never the same answer received.

Every variety observed causes you to generate the question, and to generate some kind of emotion that wants discovery of the opposite side of that emotion. In other words, some kind of discomfort that causes your discovery of more comfort is always different in nature, it is infinite.

With every question, Everything That Exists reconfigures, so you can experience more of that which you put the request for. By asking the question, you put in a request to receive and perceive more of that which is infinite, eternal bliss and ecstasy.

> ***I personally feel that I am more and more aware. But predominantly, what I am aware of is the possibilities. And that is exciting to me. But now I want to express myself more deliberately through these possibilities, and potentialities. So how do I do that?***

As you have had a predominant pattern of the question-question dance, and you move to some of the question-answer, you do not move immediately to that place of predominant experience of ease in the process. You do not see everything as a valuable reflection, and you do not accept instantaneously that everything is a reflection of you. To get there, you need constant reminders. As something resonates within you, as a potentiality, you want to revisit it, you want to stay on it and practice it.

It is not a one and done kind of process.

It does show you the potential, where you can go, but it is still not really a part of you until it's well underway. And so, it requires a certain amount of discipline and consistency.

It requires a certain amount of thirst to *experience* more of that potential, not only to understand it *intellectually*. For a while, you will see that your flashlight of attention is still in the similar place where it was before. As you continue to be more curious about this and as your awareness grows, you will start moving more towards the experiential part of it.
All you have to do is let it in.

All you have to do is let go and allow your experience to take the lead from your mind.

You cannot compute your infinite potential with your mind, you can only experience it and therefore unlock different dimensions of life.

WEOLA'S CLOSING

There was a lot of energy exchange and movement while you were reading these pages.

A truly transformational experience has taken place.

Sit with it for a moment.

Sense it.

Honor it.

Appreciate it.

Feel its vibrancy.

Sense its stillness.

Embody its steadiness.

We All Are One.

As you continue going about your integrated life experience, you will see more and more evidence of continual contribution your uniqueness brings to One.

And unconditionality that One brings to you.

And mutuality in this *eternal dance* of all of your perspectives.

In appreciation of all the asking that has brought to light the first of many materials like this,

For now,

That's it.

GLOSSARY

The Process of Channeling: A time frame when one takes their stands, opinions, beliefs, thoughts, emotions out of the equation for a moment. In other words, one can observe variety and not be caught in the judgment of it. This is to observe and then flow the energy from a Wider Perspective.

Source, God, Divine, The Universe: An undefinable, boundless, wide perspective of Everything That Exists.

Wider Perspective: You as Oneness.

Specific Perspective: You as Self.

Focus: Directing flashlight of attention outwards to observe variety.

Unfocus: Dispersing the flashlight of attention to look within.

Physical: Specific angle from which the Self perceives.

Non-physical: General angle the Self has access to at all times.

Integrated physical and non-physical: Unique vantage point, at that moment unparalleled in all existence.

Being in the question: Receiving the clarity of wanting.

Being in the answer: Receiving the wanting in physical form.

The dance between the Question and Answer: An eternal movement between desire and its realization.

The creation process: An already balanced balancing act, whether consciously perceived or not.

You are the process: You are an ever changing, ever evolving, never ending unique perspective of One.

Mind: An aspect for deciphering and a doorway for experiencing more than the Self.

Body: A physical vessel carrying out current life force experience.

Thought: The first manifestation of directing the flashlight of attention.

Emotions: A tool that shows where the Self is currently in their creation process.

Mirror reflection: The essential aspect for expansion in all dimensions.

Covering and uncovering the mirror: Putting the head in the sand to get to steady and looking to check out steadiness by observing what once was a trigger that caused putting the head in the sand to begin with.

Mutuality: Ever accurate matching game that provides, with no exception, valuable feedback.

Clarity of the question and the answer: Moments that bring desire, and a desire to desire to life respectively.

Receiving: The process of letting the Self witness in reality what once was in the form of a thought or an idea.

Meditation: A process that puts mind and body in an equanimous position, where neither of the two is more active then another, but both quiet and therefore more perceptive for different dimensions of life experience.

Expansion: Process of stretching the boundaries of physical perspective by making each next boundary fuller, wider and more inclusive.

Everything That Exists: An eternal, ever growing, never-ending wide perspective of awareness fueled by a dance between the question and the answer.

Steadiness: A dynamic position where movement feels like stillness and speed at once.

WEOLA: An acronym for We All Are One, received by Kosta & Armand to distinguish when Wider Perspective dominantly flows through Kosta during workshop gatherings.

Tools: Anything that assists the Self to get to steady.

Joy: Natural consequence, feeling when observing from the perspective of One.

Happiness: Joy perpetuated predominantly.

Ease: Moment before and after receiving the answer.

The tipping point: More or less perceived moments of switching the tides during the creation process.

Survival mode: A necessity to satisfy, so the Self can keep carrying on with its physical vessel and all its faculties.

Desire: A driving force fueled by uniqueness of a current integrated position and evolution.

State of being: Momentarily recognized, presence always in motion.

Variety: Anything the Self gives attention to, a feedback that provides Everything that Exists and physicality with eternity.

Oneness: The perspective from which differences are not perceived, a position beyond preferences, stands, opinions, beliefs, expectations, thoughts and emotions.

Consciousness: Stream of life force directed by every focusing mechanism.

Printed in Great Britain
by Amazon